COOL
CAKE TOPPERS

COOL
CAKE TOPPERS
PUT ANYTHING YOU WANT ON A CAKE

AMANDA RAWLINS & CAROLINE DEASY

Search Press

This edition published in 2012 by
Search Press Ltd
Wellwood
North Farm Road
Tunbridge Wells
Kent TN2 3DR
www.searchpress.com

A Quintet book
Copyright © 2012 Quintet Publishing Limited
All rights reserved.
QTT.CCTO

ISBN: 978-1-84448-837-7

This book was conceived, designed and produced by
Quintet Publishing Limited
6 Blundell Street
London N7 9BH

Project Editor: Lindsay Kaubi
Designer: Bonnie Bryan
Photographer: Tim Bowden
Pre-Press: Gareth Butterworth
Editorial Director: Donna Gregory
Art Director: Michael Charles
Publisher: Mark Searle

Printed in China

Contents

Directory of cake toppers 24

Introduction

As sisters, we have always shared a love of baking, since the days we baked jam tarts with our Mum. Over the years we have wowed our family and friends with our exquisite baked treats. That was until Mandy, while living in the US, discovered a passion for all things cupcake; she was amazed by how these little treasures could be transformed into objects of celebration in their own right.

On Mandy's return to the UK, we decided to turn our hobby into a business and cupcakeoccasions.co.uk was born. Cupcake Occasions has now flourished into an internationally recognised 'cupcakery', with our handmade decorations now considered an art form. We are passionate about cake decorating and relish the next cupcake experience to get our teeth into: we are both continually challenging ourselves and the boundaries of cake decoration.

We have always felt that our craft is something that can be easily taught and are surprised every time by the excitement cake decoration evokes in people, especially the achievement of producing something beautiful when you think you have no skill!

This book aims to show that making your own *Cool Cake Toppers* is very achievable!

Every baker wants to personalise their celebration cakes and *Cool Cake Toppers* will provide ideas and guidance to the amateur cake maker as well as inspiration to the professional.

Sharing our experience and the philosophy of 'we can put anything on a cupcake', this book encourages everyone to create their own quirky cake toppers by:

- Providing a summary of the materials and equipment you will need to create your cake toppers.

- Showing the different effects that can be achieved within the sugar-craft realm, including the use of sugarpaste, frosting techniques, colouring and edible and non-edible embellishments.

- Demonstrating step-by-step techniques that make it easy to produce professional-looking cake and cupcake toppers.

It's time to inspire the baker in you, awaken your inner artist and create something cool and amazing for your friends and family to delight over.

Enjoy!

Mandy and Caroline

Tools and equipment

The following equipment is recommended when baking either a 20 cm (8-inch) round cake, 12 cupcakes or 24 mini cupcakes.

BAKING EQUIPMENT

★ Cookie scoops: either 3 tablespoons (45 ml) for cupcakes or 1–1½ teaspoons (7 ml) for mini cupcakes (1)

★ Two 20 cm (8-inch) round baking tins (2)

★ 12-cup muffin pan or 24-mini-cup muffin pan (3)

★ Measuring spoons (4)

★ Cooling rack (5)

★ Cupcake cases: regular and mini sizes (6)

★ Baking parchment (7)

★ Cake board or drums that match your cake tin size

★ Stand mixer or handheld mixer

Here is a selection of the decorating tools used in this book. They are widely available from craft shops and other specialist shops. Although they are recommended, they are not essential and you can find a multitude of alternatives in your kitchen; piping tips are perfect as small circle cutters and kitchen knives as blade tools.

DECORATING TOOLS

★ Piping bags (1)

★ Piping tips (2)

★ Rolling pin (3)

★ Cutters,
   various shapes (4)

★ Craft knife (5)

★ Spatula (6)

★ Modelling tools (7)

★ Cocktail sticks/wooden
   skewers (8)

★ Edible glue (9)

★ Paintbrushes (10)

★ Sugarpaste smoother (11)

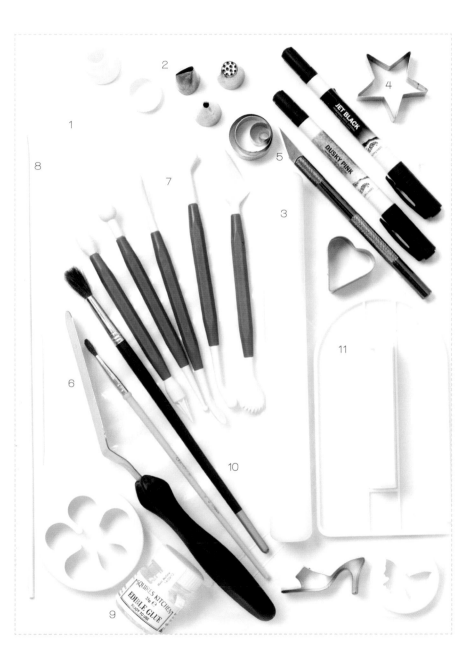

Baking
the cake

The following recipes for a vanilla sponge and a rich chocolate cake can be easily adapted to suit cakes or cupcakes. These recipes will yield enough batter for a 20 cm (8-inch) diameter cake or for 24 cupcakes. A 20 cm (8-inch) cake will feed between 12 and 15 people.

If you are not a confident baker, there is nothing wrong with using a shop-bought cake mix. A 500 g (18¼ oz) box will yield the same amount as the recipes listed here.

Ideally, the cake from this recipe should be eaten on the day it is baked, but the sponge will stay moist overnight if kept

wrapped in clingfilm. For a cake with a longer shelf life, we suggest using a shop-bought cake mix because this will yield a sponge that can last up to five days. This is ideal for cakes that need to be made ahead, like celebration or wedding cakes. This recipe calls for the use of a stand mixer or handheld mixer.

VANILLA SPONGE

INGREDIENTS

285 g (10 oz) butter, softened at room temperature

285 g (10 oz) caster sugar

1 tsp (5ml) glycerine (optional, this helps keep the cake moist)

5 large eggs

1 tsp vanilla extract

285 g (10 oz) self-raising flour

FOR VANILLA CAKE

★ Preheat the oven to 180°C (350°F) and line two 20 cm (8-inch) round cake tins with waxed paper.

★ Cream the butter, sugar and glycerine (if using) together until pale and fluffy. Beat in the eggs one at a time with a tablespoon (15 ml) of the flour and add in the vanilla extract. Mix until the ingredients are combined.

★ Add the remaining flour and beat until light and fluffy.

★ Divide between the two pans and bake for 40 minutes or until a skewer inserted into the centre of the cake comes out clean.

★ Leave to stand for 10 minutes and then turn onto a wire rack to cool.

FOR VANILLA CUPCAKES

★ Halve the above recipe to make twelve 5 cm (2-inch) cupcakes. Preheat the oven to 180°C (350°F) and line a muffin pan with 12 muffin-sized cupcake cases. Use a tablespoon to evenly distribute the batter between the cases. To ensure even-sized cupcakes, you could use a 3-tablespoon (45 ml) sized cookie scoop. The batter should come half or two thirds of the way up the cases.

★ Bake for 17 to 20 minutes.

FOR MINI VANILLA CUPCAKES

★ Quarter the original recipe to make twenty-four 3 cm (1¼-inch) mini cupcakes. Preheat the oven to 180°C (350°F) and line a mini-muffin pan with 24 mini-muffin cases. Use a 1½-teaspoon (7 ml) cookie scoop to distribute the batter between the cases to ensure even-sized cupcakes.

★ Bake for 12 to 14 minutes.

RICH CHOCOLATE CAKE

INGREDIENTS

100 g (3½ oz) cocoa powder

375 ml (1½ cups) of boiling water

190 g (6¾ oz) butter, softened at room temperature

410 g (14½ oz) caster sugar

300 g (10½ oz) plain flour

¾ tsp (4 ml) bicarbonate of soda

½ tsp (2 ml) baking powder

3 medium eggs

FOR RICH CHOCOLATE CAKE

★ Preheat the oven to 180°C (350°F).

★ Mix the cocoa powder with the boiling water and allow to cool.

★ Line two 20 cm (8-inch) round cake tins with Baking parchment.

★ Cream the butter and sugar together until pale and fluffy. Beat in the eggs, one at a time, with a tablespoon (15 ml) of the flour to avoid curdling. Mix until the ingredients are combined.

★ Add the remaining flour alternating with the cocoa mixture and then fold in the remaining ingredients until combined. Divide between the two pans and bake for 1 hour or until a skewer inserted into the middle of the cake comes out clean.

★ Leave to stand for 10 minutes and then turn out onto a wire rack to cool.

FOR RICH CHOCOLATE CUPCAKES

★ Halve the above recipe to make 12 cupcakes. Preheat the oven to 180°C (350°F) and line a muffin pan with 12 muffin-sized cupcake cases. Use a tablespoon or a 3-tablespoon (45 ml) sized cookie scoop to distribute the batter between the cases. The batter should come half or two thirds of the way up the cases.

★ Bake for 17 to 20 minutes.

FOR MINI RICH CHOCOLATE CUPCAKES

★ Quarter the original recipe to make 24 mini cupcakes. Preheat the oven to 180°C (350°F) and line a mini-muffin pan with 24 mini-muffin cases. Use a 1½ teaspoon (7 ml) cookie scoop to distribute the batter between the cases to ensure even-sized cupcakes.

★ Bake for 12 to 14 minutes.

Frosting

The following recipe will frost 24 cupcakes. You will need to halve this recipe to frost a 20 cm (8-inch) diameter cake in preparation for the sugarpaste covering.

FROSTING RECIPE

INGREDIENTS

140 g (5 oz) vegetable shortening

70 g (2½ oz) unsalted butter, softened at room temperature

1 tsp (5 ml) glycerine (optional, this helps to keep the frosting light and fluffy)

1 tbsp clear vanilla essence

340 g (12 oz) icing sugar

2–3 tbsp (30–45 ml) water

MAKING FROSTING

★ Beat the vegetable shortening, butter, vanilla essence and glycerine (if using) until light and fluffy.

★ Add the icing sugar and slowly incorporate with the other ingredients.

★ Add the water, turn up the mixer and beat on high for at least three minutes, until light and fluffy.

PREPARING A CAKE FOR SUGARPASTE

★ Even out the cake by slicing any domed tops off both cakes. Sandwich the trimmed cakes together with frosting and seedless jam, ensuring the bottom of the cake layer is facing up. You may need to trim the edges to remove any crust that may show through the sugarpaste.

★ Place the cake on a cake board or drum 2.5 cm (1 inch) bigger than the cake. Cover the cake in a thin layer of frosting, but don't worry about creating a smooth, perfect finish. This acts as a glue for the sugarpaste.

★ You can also place a table knife in a glass of freshly boiled water and skim the cake to provide an even surface.

★ Refrigerate the cake, preferably overnight, to firm up the cake and frosting.

FROSTING TECHNIQUES

These are the frosting techniques used for the designs in this book. A good tip is that it's much easier to place a piping bag in a drinking glass when filling it with frosting. No mess!

COLOURING FROSTING AND BUTTERCREAM

★ Because buttercream is cream coloured, you need to consider this when adding colouring. Using the whitest butter (unsalted butter) will result in a whiter buttercream.

★ Liquid food colouring is ideal for pastel shades, but it will not produce intense colour.

★ To create intense colours you need to use colour pastes. However, there is a warning! To obtain vibrant colours like red, black and purple, you will need to use lots of colouring to achieve the colour you require, resulting in a runnier and bitter-tasting frosting/buttercream. The other side-effect is that you may find that your guests are walking around with purple or black mouths after eating.

★ There are highly concentrated colour pastes on the market that allow you to use less paste to produce a vibrant result.

FROSTING A CUPCAKE WITH A WHIP

★ Fill a piping bag with the desired colour of frosting and use a Wilton no.1M/2110 tip.

★ To swirl the top of the cupcake, start at the back of the cupcake, swirl around the edge and then continue inwards to fill. Finally, release pressure and pull away.

★ Now pipe a smaller second ring in the centre to form a peak.

★ Add any further decorations before the frosting sets.

HAND-PIPED ROSES

★ Fill the piping bag with the desired colour of frosting and use a Wilton no. 104 petal tip.

★ You can either pipe onto a small piece of baking parchment on a piping nail and then transfer to the cake/cupcake after piping or you can pipe directly onto a cupcake.

★ Position the tip onto the centre of the nail/cupcake, with the wide end touching the base. Apply pressure and turn the nail/cupcake a complete turn until you form a cone shape.

★ Start the first petal with the wide end of the tip touching the base of the cone, then turn the nail/cupcake and gently lift and drop to form the first petal.

★ Start the second petal a third of the way back and over the first petal. Repeat the same motions as for the first petal. You should aim to have three petals around the cone.

★ Continue the petal motion until you have completed the rose.

★ The same method applies to mini cupcakes.

GRASS OR HAIR

★ Colour the frosting green, fill the piping bag and use a Wilton no. 233 multi-opening tip.

★ Practice a few strokes by applying pressure to the cake and then pulling away to create grass.

★ The same method can be used to give the effect of hair.

MULTICOLOURED FROSTING

★ This technique allows you to mix more than one frosting colour and create some cool effects, such as fire – red, yellow and orange and water – white and blue.

★ Place your piping bag with the desired tip in a drinking glass and fill each side with a different colour of frosting. Squeeze the piping bag and practise a few strokes until the colours merge.

Sugarpaste

Sugarpaste is a sugar-based icing with a dough-like consistency, which is ideal for covering cakes and modelling cake decorations. It is readily available in supermarkets in white. More colours are available from specialist shops. You can easily colour white sugarpaste with either food colouring or colour pastes. After use, if adequately wrapped, it will keep until its use-by date

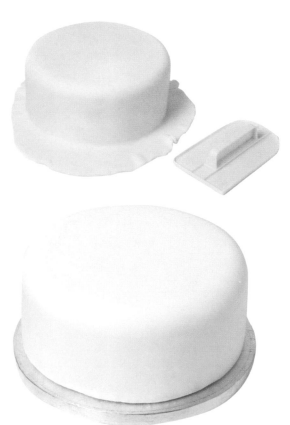

COVERING A CAKE IN SUGARPASTE

★ After frosting the cake in a thin, rough layer (see page 13), take the cake out of the fridge 30 minutes before you plan to cover with sugarpaste.

★ Lightly cover a flat surface with icing sugar and roll out 425 g (15 oz) of your desired colour of sugarpaste in a circular shape and to a thickness of 7 mm (¼ inch).

★ Lift the sugarpaste over the cake to cover it and use your hands to gently smooth the sugarpaste over the cake.

★ If there are any air bubbles, pop them with a pin and gently smooth them out with your finger.

★ Using a sugarpaste smoother, start at the top of the cake and smooth the sugarpaste to ensure a flat and even surface. Repeat on the sides of the cake. Trim any excess sugarpaste with a knife.

★ Covering a cake in sugarpaste keeps the sponge moist for up to a week after baking. This allows you to bake ahead and finish the cake decoration prior to a big event or occasion.

★ Allow to dry for 24 hours before decorating.

FLAT SUGARPASTE-COVERED CUPCAKE

★ To achieve a smooth, flat sugarpaste-covered cupcake, roll out the sugarpaste as described at left and use a 6.5 cm (2½-inch) circle cutter to cut out a circle.

★ Apply 1 tablespoon (15 ml) of frosting to the top of the cupcake. Place the circle of sugarpaste on top and smooth with the palm of your hand until flat.

COLOURING SUGARPASTE

You can easily colour white sugarpaste by using either food colouring or colour pastes.

For pastel shades, use a cocktail stick to dot the desired colour into the sugarpaste. Knead on a surface dusted with icing sugar until you reach the desired shade. You may need to add more food colouring as you work.

Alternatively, if you have sugarpaste in a primary colour, you can mix a small amount of the coloured sugarpaste with white sugarpaste to reach your desired shade.

It's just like mixing paint colours:
Pink = white + red
Lemon = white + yellow
Lilac = white + grape
Tan = white + brown or chocolate-flavored sugarpaste

To mix stronger colours yourself, it's best to use colouring paste.

COLOUR EFFECTS

The versatility of sugarpaste allows you to mix a number of colours to create some exciting effects.

Water = white + pale blue + blue
Marble = white + small amount of black
Wood = brown + small amount of tan
Parchment = tan + small amount of brown

Roll the colours into equal length sausages and then roll together, bend in half and press together; repeat the process until you reach the desired effect. The key is not to over-mix the sugarpaste to blend the colours. Roll out the sugarpaste and use as directed.

MAKING CAKE AND CUPCAKE TOPPERS FROM SUGARPASTE

Do you remember modelling dough when you were a child? Sugarpaste is exactly the same! You can create almost anything from sugarpaste. It is ideal for cake decorations because it is pliable and is hard enough to support itself when dry.

MODELLING

To make the sugarpaste pliable, knead it on a surface dusted with icing sugar or cornflour. You can then mould it or roll it out to cut out decorations freehand or with cutters. For the decorations in this book you should roll the sugarpaste to 2 mm ($^1/_{16}$ inch) thick unless otherwise directed.

TEMPLATES

A number of templates are supplied on pages 140–141. These can be photocopied and cut out with scissors. You can then place the template on the rolled sugarpaste and cut around it with a craft knife. You can tidy the edges of your cutout with either the edge of the knife or your finger. If the recipe calls for a cutter that you do not have, you can always make your own template or try and cut it out free-handed.

CUTTERS

There is a vast array of cutters available in both supermarkets and specialist shops and you will probably already have a few in your kitchen drawers. You can also be imaginative with other tools and equipment you have in your kitchen; piping tips are perfect for small circles and drinking glasses for larger circles.

DRYING

Once you have made your decoration, lay it on Baking parchment on a flat surface. Most decorations call for a 24-hour drying time, but many will probably support their own weight after just a few hours. Once dry, your decorations will keep for at least two weeks, which is ideal when you are creating a celebration cake and cupcakes and want to get ahead, instead of creating a masterpiece on the morning of the event!

FRILLING

Frilling is good for creating skirts, blankets and other fabrics. It is also used in the rosette (see page 118). Placing a skewer over the edge of the sugarpaste where the taper of the skewer starts and gently rolling it along the sugarpaste achieves this effect.

Decorations

There are many ways to embellish your cakes and cupcakes. Here are some of the options available, but the key is to use these techniques with your imagination to create fabulous and individual toppers!

SUGARPASTE

This is ideal for rolling flat, cutting out decorations and moulding. When dried hard, the sugarpaste decorations will stand up on the cake and cupcakes to achieve a great three-dimensional effect.

GUM PASTE

This can be used as an alternative to sugarpaste for modelling, as it dries harder. Although edible, it is not palatable. It's ideal for cake toppers, but we would not recommend its use in cupcake decorations.

MARZIPAN OR ALMOND PASTE

This can be used as an alternative to sugarpaste and is commonly used to mould fruits and vegetables. It can be a tastier option for larger edible decorations.

PIPING EFFECTS

The frosting recipe on page 13 can be used with a piping bag and tip (or tips) to create many three-dimensional effects, including roses, grass, hair, leaves and lettering.

SWEETS, DRAGÉES AND SPRINKLES

Ideal for small details such as eyes and noses. Sweets can also be rolled out to achieve a new medium.

GLITTERS

Edible glitter adds a sparkle to decorations or frosting.

LUSTRE SPRAY

This is used to create a pearlised, gold or silver finish.

EDIBLE INKS AND PAINTS

Edible-ink pens can be used to easily draw or write on hardened sugarpaste. Paint lustres can be mixed with a clear alcohol, like white rum or vodka and painted onto decorations. The alcohol then evaporates and leaves a painted finish.

OTHER EDIBLES

Cookie crumbs can be used to create sand and dirt effects; chocolate sticks and wafer rolls can be used for structural strength when required.

NON-EDIBLE ALTERNATIVES

Use custom-printed and laminated toppers for a personalised effect. It's easy to craft personalised cupcake toppers using a computer, then print and laminate the results. Laminating ensures that they are food safe, but you should make your guests aware that they are not edible. You can personalise them with names, ages, favourite characters and even photos. The possibilities are endless!

You can also enhance your cakes with shop-bought cake toppers. Diamanté initials and brooches provide a classy effect, as do feathers and small bouquets of flowers.

Whether you wish to decorate cupcakes for a school cake sale or create a wedding extravaganza, the designs in the Directory of cake toppers will be the centre of attention. They are aimed at all levels of experience and are demonstrated step by step to make creating fantastic cake toppers easy.

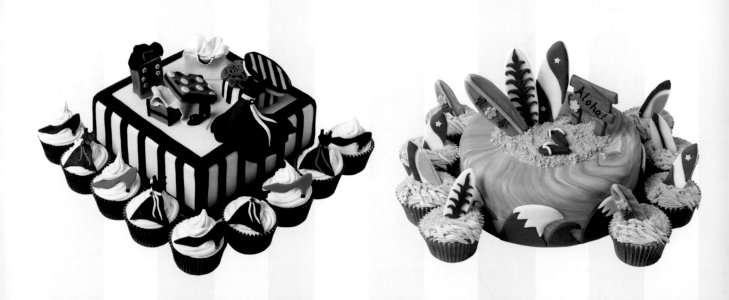

Directory of cake toppers

BUTTONS THE BEAR

If you go down to the woods today, you're sure of a big surprise! This cuddly fella is ready for a big hug!

TOOLS AND MATERIALS

Knife or blade tool and rolling pin

Skewer and cocktail stick or modelling tool

Tan and white sugarpastes

Any metal piping tip

Edible glue and brush

NOTES ON THE CAKE

A 15 cm (6-inch) cake covered in white sugarpaste was used for this design. Handmade tan sugarpaste buttons in two sizes were glued around the base of the cake.

THE BEAR

HOW TO MAKE

STEP 1

★ Roll out a 3 cm (1¼-inch) ball of tan sugarpaste for the body and mould into shape.

★ Roll a 2.5 cm (1-inch) ball for the head and two 2 cm (¾-inch) balls for the arms and legs. Cut the balls for the arms and legs in half to ensure you have an equal amount of sugarpaste for each one.

★ Roll out two 7 mm (¼-inch) balls for the ears.

★ Roll out a 1.5 cm (½-inch) white sugarpaste ball for the snout.

STEP 2

★ Flatten out the white sugarpaste ball for the snout and use the bottom of a metal piping tip to indent the mouth.

★ Roll out the arms and the legs and use the flat end of a skewer to indent the paws on the bottom of the feet.

★ Roll the ears into teardrop shapes and use the end of the skewer or modelling stick to indent the ears and then pinch the end of the teardrop shape together to make a point.

STEP 3

★ Use the skewer or modelling tool to make two holes in the top of the head and glue the ears into position. Glue the snout onto the head and use a cocktail stick to mark the eyes. Model a small piece of tan sugarpaste for the nose and glue in place.

★ Sit the body upright and glue the arms and legs in place.

★ Insert a cocktail stick into the body and secure the head in position; make sure your protruding cocktail stick is not longer than the head.

★ To make the buttons, take two small white sugarpaste balls, flatten them down with the flat end of the skewer and prick four holes with the cocktail stick. Glue to the bear's tummy.

From baby showers to the new arrival, these adorable cupcakes will have everyone cooing!

TOOLS AND MATERIALS

Knife or blade tool and rolling pin

3 cm (1¼-inch) and 2.5 cm (1-inch) circle cutter for the pram

7 mm (¼-inch) and 8 mm (⅓-inch) circle cutters

Pale pink sugarpaste

White or pearl dragées

Edible glue and brush

THE PRAM

HOW TO MAKE

STEP 1

★ Roll out the pale pink sugarpaste and cut out a 3 cm (1¼-inch) circle. Using the 2.5 cm (1-inch) circle cutter, indent the larger circle.

★ Roll out two 7 mm (¼-inch) balls of pink sugarpaste and press with your finger to create two 1.5 cm (½-inch) circles for the wheels.

STEP 2

★ Cut out a triangle from the 3 cm (1¼-inch) circle, between one and three o'clock. Using a 7mm (¼-inch) circle cutter, cut out two wheel arches at the base. Roll between your fingers to create a pram handle.

★ Using the blade tool or knife, indent the hood of the pram and using the 8 mm (⅓-inch) circle cutter, indent the wheels.

★ Glue the parts together and then glue two white dragées into the centre of the wheels.

STEP 3

★ Allow to dry for 12 hours and place on a frosted cupcake.

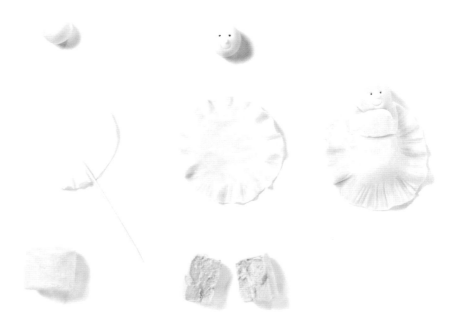

TOOLS AND MATERIALS

Knife or blade tool and rolling pin

5.5 cm (2¼-inch) circle cutter

Cocktail stick, skewer and piping nozzle

Marshmallows

Skin-coloured sugarpaste

Pale pink sugarpaste

Edible glue and brush

BABES IN BLANKET

HOW TO MAKE

STEP 1

★ For the blanket, roll out the pale pink sugarpaste and cut out a 5.5 cm (2¼-inch) circle. Take a skewer, place it on the edge of the blanket and gently roll up and down to create the frill detail (see page 19).

★ Roll a ball of skin-coloured sugarpaste that is 2 cm (¾-inch) in diameter.

STEP 2

★ Mark eyes with a cocktail stick and indent for the mouth with a piping nozzle. Add a small ball of sugarpaste for the nose.

★ Cut the marshmallow in half lengthwise.

STEP 3

★ Lay the blanket over the half marshmallow, add the baby's head and assemble on the cupcake.

SPOTTY DUCK

This delightful duck is an ideal topper for all things baby: baby showers, new baby, christenings.

TOOLS AND MATERIALS

Knife or blade tool and rolling pin

Pale blue, white and yellow sugarpaste

No. 5 piping tube or 3 mm (⅛-inch) circle cutter

Cocktail stick

Edible glue and brush

NOTES ON THE CAKE

A 15 cm (6-inch) cake covered in white sugarpaste, with a coordinating spotty satin ribbon around the base was used here.

THE DUCK

HOW TO MAKE

STEP 1

★ Roll out a 4 cm (1½-inch) ball of pale blue sugarpaste for the body and a 2.5 cm (1-inch) ball for the head.

STEP 2

★ Roll the larger ball at one end and pinch flat to create the tail.

★ Use a cocktail stick to create the eyes on the head. Make a small triangle of yellow sugarpaste for the beak and then fix in place with a little edible glue.

★ Glue the head to the body.

STEP 3

★ Cut out the white spots using the piping tube or circle cutter and glue in place.

★ Allow to dry for at least 12 hours.

BABY NAME BLOCKS

These brightly colored play blocks are ideal for a child's christening or first birthday party.

TOOLS AND MATERIALS

Knife or blade tool and rolling pin

7 ounces (200 g) white fondant (makes five blocks)

Tan, yellow, green, blue and red fondants

Small alphabet cutters, less than 1-inch (2.5 cm) square

Selection of small object cutters, less than 1-inch (2.5 cm) square

Edible glue and brush

NOTES ON THE CAKE

A 6-inch (15 cm) round cake covered in tan fondant was used. A red gingham ribbon was tied around the middle with a bow. Secure the bow in place with a pin. Make sure that the pin is removed before serving.

THE NAME BLOCKS

HOW TO MAKE

STEP 1

★ Using a large kitchen knife and white fondant, create a three-dimensional rectangle that is 1-inch (2.5 cm) square and 5-inch (12.5 cm) long. Cut out 1-inch (2.5 cm) cubes for the required number of letter blocks. To make the edges sharper, pinch with your fingers and flatten the sides with a large knife or cake smoother.

STEP 3

★ Glue the letters to the top of the blocks and the objects around the sides.

★ Secure to the top of the cake with either a cocktail stick or edible glue.

STEP 2

★ Indent each face of the cube with a square border using the blade tool.

★ Roll out the coloured sugarpastes to 1.5 mm (1/16-inch) thickness and cut out your required name with small alphabet cutters in a mixture of sugarpaste colours.

★ Use a selection of small object cutters to decorate your blocks, for example, teddy bear, stars, hearts and butterflies. Or you can cut them out by hand.

NAUTICAL NAME CAKE

Land ahoy! Navigate your little sailor with the aid of this charming nautical-themed cake, ideal for a christening or naming ceremony.

TOOLS AND MATERIALS

Knife or blade tool and rolling pin

Skewer and cocktail stick

Baby blue, white, red and black sugarpastes

5 cm (2-inch) circle cutter

1 cm (½-inch) and 7 mm (¼-inch) circle cutters

Small star cutter

Star sprinkles

Edible glue and brush

NOTES ON THE CAKE

A 20 cm (8-inch) round cake covered in pale blue sugarpaste was used. A red-striped nautical ribbon was wrapped around the base and secured with a pin at the back and a life preserver decoration added to the front. Marble sugarpaste rocks were placed around the lighthouse (see page 17).

Covering cake drums and cake spacers with coloured paper and hot-gluing them together created the cake stand and the edges were trimmed with satin ribbon. This is a great way to create a customised stand.

THE LIGHTHOUSE

HOW TO MAKE

STEP 1

★ Roll a 5 cm (2-inch) ball of white sugarpaste and model into a lighthouse shape, 7.5 cm (3 inches) high.

★ Using red sugarpaste, cut out three strips that measure 11.5 x 1.5 cm (4½ x ½ inches). Glue one at the top of the lighthouse, one at the bottom and one halfway up and cut each strip to length.

STEP 2

★ Cut out a 4 cm (1½-inch) white sugarpaste circle and glue to the top of the lighthouse.

★ Create the light from grey sugarpaste. It should be a cylinder 1.5 cm (½ inch) in diameter by 2 cm (¾ inch) long. Indent a criss-cross pattern on it with a blade tool and glue in place. Cut out a 3 mm (⅛-inch) strip of red sugarpaste and glue around the light.

★ Mould a cone to fit on top of the light and indent rings using a circle cutter. Top off with a small rolled ball of sugarpaste.

★ Cut out two windows and a door from black sugarpaste and glue in place.

★ Insert a cocktail stick into the base of the lighthouse and leave to dry for 24 hours.

THE BOAT

HOW TO MAKE

STEP 1

★ Roll and cut out a 4 cm (1½-inch) high white sugarpaste triangle for the sail, then roll out and cut out a baby blue triangle sail. Glue the sails to a cocktail stick.

★ Roll and cut out two red sugarpaste stripes and glue to the blue sail. Glue a red star sprinkle to the white sail.

★ Roll and cut out a three-dimensional hull shape that is 2.5 cm (1 inch) long from the red sugarpaste.

STEP 2

★ Cut out a small red circle and a small white circle. Cut the red circle into eight parts and glue four of the parts onto the white circle to create a life buoy.

>

THE BUNTING CUPCAKE

HOW TO MAKE

★ Flat-sugarpaste a cupcake with baby blue sugarpaste as shown on page 17.

★ Roll out some white sugarpaste and cut out a triangle to fit on your cupcake.

★ Roll out some red sugarpaste and cut out the required letter and a strip for the bunting ribbon.

★ Glue the triangle, letter and ribbon to the frosted cupcake and use the end of a sharp knife to indent a stitching pattern.

THE BOAT CUPCAKE TOPPER

HOW TO MAKE

★ Roll out and cut a white sugarpaste triangle sail that is 4 cm (1½ inches) high, then roll out and cut out a baby blue triangle sail.

★ Roll out the red sugarpaste and cut out a flat hull shape that is 2.5 cm (1 inch) long.

★ Roll out and cut two red sugarpaste stripes and glue to the blue sail. Glue a red star sprinkle to the white sail.

THE LIGHTHOUSE
CUPCAKE TOPPER

HOW TO MAKE

★ Cut out a lighthouse shape from white sugarpaste that is 2.5 cm (1 inch) high.

★ Cut a triangle roof from red sugarpaste.

★ Cut three red strips and glue into position.

★ Cut a door and window from black sugarpaste and glue in place.

THE ANCHOR
CUPCAKE TOPPER

HOW TO MAKE

★ Roll a baby blue sausage shape for the main shank.

★ Mould an arc for the base and glue to the shank.

★ Cut a small ball in half, roll each one and glue to the main shank.

★ Roll a thin sausage, curl it round to make the top ring and glue in place.

ENCHANTED GARDEN

Tiptoe into an enchanted land where these magical creatures dwell!

TOOLS AND MATERIALS

Knife or blade tool and rolling pin

Pale blue, pale yellow, pale pink, red and white fondants

Toothpick and any metal piping tip

Small flower cutter

Edible glitter

Edible glue and brush

CORY THE CATERPILLAR

HOW TO MAKE

STEP 1

★ Roll four ½-inch (1.5 cm) balls of pale blue fondant.

★ Roll an ⅛-inch (3 mm) ball of blue fondant and cut in half.

★ To create the mushroom, roll out a ½-inch (1.5 cm) ball of red fondant and a ball of white fondant.

STEP 2

★ Glue the four blue balls together to create the caterpillar, mark his eyes with a toothpick and make an indent for his mouth with a piping tip.

★ To make the feelers, roll the small blue halves of fondant into thin sausages.

★ To create the top of the mushroom, use a ball tool to press the red fondant ball into the palm of your hand. Roll the white fondant into a cone shape to create the mushroom stalk.

STEP 3

★ Use a toothpick to create a hole in the caterpillar's head for the feelers and glue them in.

★ Roll small balls of white fondant and glue them to the top of the mushroom. Glue the top of the mushroom to the stalk.

SALLY THE SNAIL

HOW TO MAKE

STEP 1

★ Roll the yellow fondant into a sausage about 6 inches (15 cm) long and ¼ inch (7 mm) thick. Smooth half of the sausage flat with your finger and, starting from the thinner end, curl it around itself to create the shell.

★ Create the head and body from pink fondant and prick two eyes and an indent for the mouth with a piping tip.

★ For the feelers, roll two small pink sausages and indent halfway with a skewer.

STEP 2

★ Glue the shell to the body and trim any excess with a knife.

★ Make a hole with a toothpick for the feelers and glue in place.

★ Use a small flower cutter to create flowers in pink fondant, and attach a small ball of yellow fondant to the centers with glue.

STEP 3

★ Frost the cupcake with grass using green buttercream and a grass tip (see page 15).

★ Assemble the creatures, mushrooms and flowers and sprinkle with magic dust (edible glitter)!

VERITY THE FAIRY

Verity is a special little fairy who lives in an enchanted garden. If you are lucky, she may grant you a wish!

TOOLS AND MATERIALS

Knife or blade tool and rolling pin

Cocktail sticks and skewer or no.3 modelling tool

Purple, pink, skin colour, yellow, white and green sugarpastes

Butterfly and 7 mm (¼-inch) flower cutter

Any metal piping tube

Edible glue and brush

NOTES ON THE CAKE

A 15 cm (6-inch) cake, covered in green sugarpaste was used for this design. Green frosting was piped around the base using the grass technique (see page 15) and some flowers were also added. The grass frosting was also used to affix Verity and the mushrooms to the top of the cake.

VERITY

HOW TO MAKE

STEP 1

★ Roll out a 2.5 cm (1-inch) ball of skin-coloured sugarpaste for the body and mould into shape. Allow to dry for an hour.

★ Roll a 2 cm (¾-inch) ball for the head and two 1 cm (½-inch) balls for the arms and legs. Cut each of these in half to ensure you have an equal amount of sugarpaste for each one. Mould into shape.

★ Roll out the purple sugarpaste and cut out a 7.5 cm (3-inch) diameter circle.

★ Roll out the pink sugarpaste and cut out the butterfly wings.

STEP 3

★ To make the top of the mushroom, use a ball tool to press a pink sugarpaste ball into the palm of your hand. Roll some white sugarpaste into a cone shape to create the mushroom stalk.

★ Roll small balls of white sugarpaste and glue to the top of the mushroom. Glue the top of the mushroom to the stalk.

★ Cut out three green sugarpaste leaves. Place cocktail sticks on the bottom quarter of the leaves, gently pinch the sugarpaste over the cocktail stick and leave to dry for 24 hours.

★ When the fairy and leaves are dry, assemble on the cake.

STEP 2

★ Sit the body upright and glue the legs into position.

★ Place the purple sugarpaste circle over the body and smooth down to make the dress.

★ Glue the arms into position and fix the butterfly wings to Verity's back.

★ Insert a cocktail stick into the fairy and place the head onto the cocktail stick.

★ Use a cocktail stick to mark the eyes and a piping tube to indent the mouth; roll a small piece of sugarpaste for the nose and glue in place.

★ Roll out long, thin sausage shapes from yellow sugarpaste and glue to the fairy's head as hair.

★ Cut out small flowers and glue to the hair.

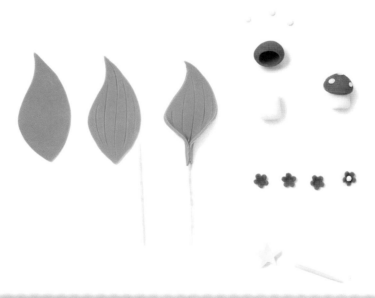

DIGGER, TRACTOR AND FIRE ENGINE

Vroom! Take a ride with every boy's favourite vehicles to do some digging, ploughing or putting out fires!

TOOLS AND MATERIALS

Knife or blade tool and a rolling pin

Yellow, grey, black, green and red sugarpastes

2.5 cm (1-inch) circle cutter

Edible glue and brush

Black edible-ink pen

THE DIGGER

HOW TO MAKE

STEP 1

★ Cut a 5 cm (2-inch) by 7 mm (¼-inch) rectangle of yellow sugarpaste and create an indent at the top.

★ Cut out a 2.5 cm (1-inch) circle from the yellow sugarpaste and cut again to create a crescent for the digger bucket. Cut a small 2.5 cm (1-inch) by 7 mm (¼-inch) strip to create the roof and two 2.5 cm (1-inch) by 3 mm (⅛-inch) strips to make wings.

STEP 2

★ Cut a 2.5 cm (1-inch) square of grey sugarpaste for the cab and a small square for the engine (indent with the knife).

★ Roll two 1 cm (½-inch) black sugarpaste balls and two 7 mm (¼-inch) yellow sugarpaste balls. Press each of the yellow sugarpaste balls into the black balls to create two wheels. Attach the yellow wings to the top of the wheels.

STEP 3

★ Glue all the parts together. Attach the bucket and digger with a strip of yellow sugarpaste.

★ Allow to dry. Place carefully on top of a whip-frosted cupcake.

THE TRACTOR

HOW TO MAKE

STEP 1

★ Cut a green sugarpaste rectangle 5 cm (2 inches) by 2.5 cm (1 inch) to create the tractor base. Cut another for the roof that is 2.5 cm (1 inch) by 7 mm (¼ inch) and two 2.5 cm (1-inch) by 3 mm (⅛-inch) strips for the wings.

★ Cut a 2.5 cm (1-inch) square from grey sugarpaste to create the window. Cut a small rectangle and indent with a knife to create the engine.

STEP 2

★ As you did for the digger, create the wheels with one 2 cm (¾-inch) black ball and one 1.5 cm (½-inch) black ball. Insert with 7 mm (¼-inch) yellow balls.

★ Glue the wings to the tops of the wheels.

STEP 3

★ Glue all of the parts together.

★ Allow to dry. Place carefully on top of a whip-frosted cupcake.

THE FIRE ENGINE

HOW TO MAKE

STEP 1

★ Cut a 5 cm (2-inch) by 3 cm (1¼-inch) rectangle of red sugarpaste and cut out an indent to create a cab shape at the front.

★ Roll three 7 mm (¼-inch) black balls to create wheels with 3 mm (⅛-inch) grey sugarpaste wheel inserts.

STEP 2

★ Cut out a small black rectangle for the cab window.

★ Cut one small square and a small rectangle in grey sugarpaste and indent with a knife to create engines and drawers.

★ Cut a 3 cm (1¼-inch) yellow strip and indent to create the ladder.

STEP 3

★ Glue the parts together.

★ Allow to dry before placing on top of a frosted cupcake.

BOBO
THE CLOWN

Roll up! Roll up! It will be smiles around with this lovable clown.

TOOLS AND MATERIALS

Knife or blade tool and rolling pin

Skewer and cocktail stick or no.3 modelling tool

Blue, green, white, red orange and yellow sugarpastes

Edible glue and brush

Any metal piping tip

Sugar-craft wire

7 mm (¼-inch) flower cutter

3 cm (1¼-inch) circle cutter

NOTES ON THE CAKE

A 15 cm (6-inch) round cake covered in white sugarpaste was used. A rainbow ribbon was placed around the base and secured at the back with a pin. Always remove any pins before serving.

BOBO

HOW TO MAKE

STEP 1

★ In blue sugarpaste, roll a 2.5 cm (1-inch) ball for the body and two 1.5 cm (½-inch) balls for the arms and legs. Cut each of these in half to ensure you have an equal amount of sugarpaste for each one. Roll a thin sausage for the hat trim.

★ Roll a 2 cm (¾-inch) green sugarpaste ball for the hat.

★ Roll a 2.5 cm (1-inch) white sugarpaste ball for the head.

★ Roll two 7 mm (¼-inch) orange sugarpaste balls for the hair.

★ Roll out a 1.5 cm (½-inch) red sugarpaste ball for the feet and cut in half. Roll four 7 mm (¼-inch) red sugarpaste balls for the pom-poms and nose.

★ Roll out and cut a 3 cm (1¼-inch) green sugarpaste circle for the ruffle.

STEP 2

★ Roll the body into shape and the arms into sausage shapes. Lay the half balls for the legs on their flat-cut sides and twist to create the legs.

★ For the feet, roll the two halves into teardrop shapes, flatten out the pointed ends with your finger and cut the point away with the round cutter.

★ Take a skewer and make the ruffle using the frilling technique shown on page 19.

★ Use a cocktail stick to mark the eyes in the head and the metal piping tip base to indent for the mouth.

★ Roll the green sugarpaste ball into a cone for the hat.

★ Roll the orange sugarpaste balls into sausages and use a blade tool to mark the hair.

STEP 3

★ Glue the hat to the head, attach the hat trim and glue the hair in place.

★ Glue the arms to the body and insert a cocktail stick halfway into the body. You can now use this to hold your clown while you glue the ruffle and head into position.

★ Glue on the nose and pom-poms.

★ Roll out and cut out a small flower from yellow sugarpaste. Add a small red ball to the centre of the flower and glue to Bobo's hat.

★ To make the balloon, roll a yellow sugarpaste ball and flatten it with your finger. Bend the wire and insert gently into the balloon. Leave to dry.

★ Use a piece of the wire to make a hole through the body (which will later hold the balloon and wire). Keep it close to the arm to prevent the wire from falling back.

★ When everything has dried, insert the cocktail stick in the clown's body between the feet and into the cake so that the stick and the legs support the body.

★ Insert the balloon wire through the hole in the body and place on top of the cake.

FARM

Create this fabulous farm cake in two shakes of a lamb's tail!

TOOLS AND MATERIALS

Knife or craft knife and rolling pin

White, pink, black, yellow, red, brown and orange sugarpastes

4.5 cm (1¾-inch) circle cutter

4.5 cm (1¾-inch) scalloped circle cutter

7 mm (¼-inch) and 3 mm (⅛-inch) flower cutters

Skewer or cocktail stick

Edible glue and brush

NOTES ON THE CAKE

A 20 cm (8-inch) round cake covered in pastel green sugarpaste was used. The fence was created using wood effect sugarpaste (see page 17). Some animal cupcake toppers were added to the sides of the cake.

The base was piped with green frosting using a grass effect (see page 14). Marble sugarpaste stones and flowers were added for decoration.

Shredded wheat was used to make the hay bales and the pond was modelled using water-effect sugarpaste (see page 17). Green frosting with a grass-effect was piped around the edge.

THE PIG CUPCAKE

HOW TO MAKE

★ Roll out the pink sugarpaste to 3 mm (⅛ inch) thick and cut out a 4.5 cm (1¾-inch) diameter circle.

★ Also in pink, roll out a 7 mm (¼-inch) ball for the snout and a 3 mm (⅛-inch) ball, which will form the ears.

★ Press the snout ball with your finger and use a skewer to mark the nose and a metal piping tip to mark the mouth.

★ Cut the ear sugarpaste into two and roll into balls. Flatten with your finger and pinch each end to create an ear. Repeat with the other half.

★ Glue the parts together, add two small black sugarpaste balls as eyes and thinly rolled pink sugarpaste for the hair.

THE HORSE CUPCAKE

HOW TO MAKE

★ Roll out the brown sugarpaste to 3 mm (⅛ inch) thick, cut out a 7 mm (¼-inch) diameter circle for the snout and mark the nose and mouth as for the pig.

★ Roll out two 7 mm (¼-inch) balls of brown sugarpaste and two 3 mm (⅛-inch) balls of pink sugarpaste. Flatten the pink sugarpaste ball on top of the brown sugarpaste ball with your finger and pinch each end to create an ear. Repeat with the other half.

★ Cut out a small triangle of tan sugarpaste and cut triangles from the base to create the mane. Cut a thin triangle from white sugarpaste to match the face markings.

★ Glue all of the parts together and add two small black sugarpaste balls for eyes.

THE DUCK CUPCAKE

HOW TO MAKE

★ Roll out the yellow sugarpaste and cut out a 4.5 cm (1¾-inch) circle. Roll out a small amount of orange sugarpaste and cut out a beak shape – do this by using the 4.5 cm (1¾-inch) circle cutter to cut a wedge from the orange sugarpaste circle. You should be left with a triangle with curving edges. Roll two thin sausages of yellow sugarpaste for the hair.

★ Glue all the parts together and add two small black sugarpaste balls for the eyes.

THE CHICKEN CUPCAKE

HOW TO MAKE

★ Roll out the white and red sugarpaste to 3 mm (⅛ inch) thick. Cut out a 4.5 cm (1¾-inch) circle from the white and, using the 4.5 cm (1¾-inch) scalloped cutter as the edge, cut out a comb and wattle from the red sugarpaste.

★ Roll out a small piece of yellow sugarpaste and cut out two small diamond shapes, one bigger than the other, for the beak. Glue all of the parts together and add two small black sugarpaste balls for the eyes.

THE COW CUPCAKE

HOW TO MAKE

★ Roll out the white sugarpaste to 3 mm (⅛ inch) thick and cut out a 4.5 cm (1¾-inch) circle.

★ In pink sugarpaste, roll a 1 cm (½-inch) ball for the snout and mark two nostrils with a skewer. Cut out a tiny 3 mm (⅛-inch) flower in yellow sugarpaste and attach as the mouth. Create the ears using white and pink sugarpaste balls.

★ Roll out the black sugarpaste and cut out a 7 mm (¼-inch) flower as the hair. Using the 4.5 cm (1¾-inch) scalloped circle cutter, cut out the various face markings.

★ Glue all the parts together and add two small black sugarpaste balls as eyes.

THE SHEEP CUPCAKE

HOW TO MAKE

★ Roll out the white sugarpaste to 3 mm (⅛ inch) thick and, using a 4.5 cm (1¾ inch) scalloped circle cutter, cut out the face. Also cut out a 1 cm (½ inch) flower for the hair. Roll out a small amount of pink sugarpaste, cut out a 1 cm (½ inch) flower for the nose and mark the nostrils with a skewer.

★ Roll out a 1 cm (½ inch) ball of white sugarpaste and a 3 mm (⅛ inch) ball of black sugarpaste. Flatten the black into the white ball with your finger. Cut the circle in half and pinch the flat edge together to create an ear. Repeat with the other half.

★ Glue all the parts together and add two small black sugarpaste balls as eyes.

THE CHICKEN

HOW TO MAKE

★ Roll a 2 cm (¾-inch) ball of white sugarpaste for the body and a 1 cm (½-inch) ball for the head. Mould the body with a tail and cut two triangles out of the tail to create feathers.

★ Using yellow sugarpaste, mould a small triangular beak and glue to the head. Create two eyes using a cocktail stick.

★ Roll out two small red sugarpaste balls, mould a wattle and comb and glue to the head. Glue the head to the body and place on a nest made of shredded wheat.

THE DUCK

HOW TO MAKE

★ Roll out two small 7 mm (¼-inch) and 1.5 cm (½-inch) balls of yellow sugarpaste. Mould the larger ball as the duck's body along with the tail. Glue the head in place and add two eyes with a cocktail stick. Mould a small beak from orange sugarpaste and glue in place.

★ Roll out a 7 mm (¼-inch) ball of yellow sugarpaste and press with your finger. Cut in half and glue to the side of the duck's body as wings. ➤

49

THE BARN

HOW TO MAKE

★ Mix some brown and red sugarpastes to create a rust colour and roll out to 7 mm (¼ inch) thick. Cut out a rectangle that is 10 x 7.5 cm (4 x 3 inches). Cut the top quarter portion to create the Dutch roof effect as shown. Use the knife and cocktail stick to create a wood-panelled effect.

★ Roll out some white sugarpaste to 7 mm (¼ inch) thick, cut out 7 mm (¼-inch) strips and glue to the side of the barn, allowing the roof to overlap to create eaves. Roll out the black sugarpaste, cut a 7 mm (¼-inch) wide strip and glue to form the roof.

★ To create the barn door, roll out the white sugarpaste to 3 mm (⅛ inch) thick and cut a 7 mm (¼-inch) wide strip. Use this strip to create a square box with a cross inside and glue to the front of the barn.

★ To create the window, roll out the black sugarpaste and cut out a rectangle that is 2.5 x 4 cm (1 x 1½ inches) and trim with thin strips of white sugarpaste. Glue in place.

THE WEATHER VANE

HOW TO MAKE

STEP 1

★ Using black sugarpaste, roll a 7 mm (¼-inch) ball for the head and a 1 cm (½-inch) ball for the body. Mould the body with a tail and cut two triangles out of the tail to create feathers.

★ Mould a small beak and comb, glue to the rooster's head and then glue the head to the body.

★ Roll one small sausage from black sugarpaste and insert the cocktail stick through it. Cut two 2 cm (¾ inch) wide strips to form the cross at the base of the weather vane. Insert the cocktail stick through the centre of the cross and attach it to the base of the rooster.

★ Assemble the weather vane on a skewer first. First add one of the small balls, then add the cross with, then the other small ball and then the rooster. Insert into some spare sugarpaste and allow to dry for 24 hours. Insert into the top of the barn before assembling on the cake.

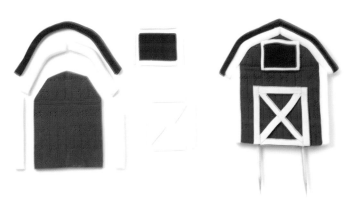

PIRATE TREASURE ISLAND

Come aboard with these swashbuckling pirates and bag yourself some treasure!

TOOLS AND MATERIALS

Knife or craft knife and rolling pin

Black, white, yellow and red sugarpastes

Wood-effect sugarpaste (see page 17)

3.5 cm (1⅓-inch) and 7.5 cm (3-inch) circle cutters

Black edible-ink pen

Edible gold paint and brush

Clear alcohol (white rum or vodka)

Round yellow sprinkles

White ball sprinkles

Gold foil chocolate coins

NOTES ON THE CAKE

A 20 cm (8-inch) round cake covered with parchment-effect sugarpaste (see page 17) was used here. The sugarpaste on the cake was left to dry for 24 hours and then a compass and treasure map details were drawn on the cake in black edible ink. The chest is placed on a pile of digestive crumbs and the base is surrounded with black sugarpaste cannonballs.

THE TREASURE CHEST

HOW TO MAKE

STEP 1

★ Using the wood-effect sugarpaste, cut three rectangles that are 2.5 x 6.5 cm (1 x 2½ inches), for the base, front and back of the chest.

★ Cut out one rectangle that is 4 cm x 6.5 cm (1½ x 2½ inches), for the lid and two 2.5 cm (1-inch) squares for the chest ends.

★ Cut a 3.5 cm (1⅓-inch) diameter circle and cut it in two for the lid ends.

★ Lay the largest rectangle (the lid) over a rolling pin and allow to set overnight.

★ After the other parts have dried for 15 minutes, glue the box together and allow to dry overnight.

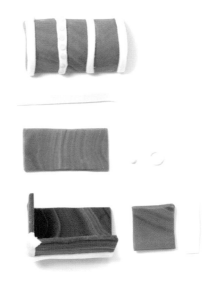

STEP 2

★ Roll out the yellow sugarpaste, cut out 7 mm (¼-inch) strips and glue to the edges of the treasure chest. Glue on round yellow sprinkles as the rivets.

★ Paint the yellow edging with gold edible paint.

STEP 3

★ Using yellow sugarpaste, mould a keyhole and two handles for each end of the chest. Dot the keyhole with black edible ink and glue to the chest.

★ When dry, fill the chest with gold chocolate coins and a pearl necklace made out of a thin sausage of white sugarpaste with white ball sprinkles glued on. The chest is ready to place on top of your cake.

THE GOLD BOOTY CUPCAKES

HOW TO MAKE

★ Simply add gold foil chocolate coins to frosted cupcakes and sprinkle with edible gold glitter.

THE SKULL AND CROSSBONES CUPCAKES

HOW TO MAKE

STEP 1

★ Roll out the black sugarpaste and cut out a 7.5 cm (3-inch) diameter circle.

★ Roll out the white sugarpaste and cut out the pirate skull using the template on page 141. Using a skewer, poke out the skull's eyes and nose. Use the knife to indent the teeth.

STEP 2

★ From the rolled white sugarpaste, cut four 7 mm x 2 cm (¼ x ¾ inch) strips. Cut the tip of one end of a sugarpaste strip and press with your finger to form the bones. Repeat this with all of the strips.

STEP 3

★ Glue the skull to the black disk and glue the four bones around the skull, trimming any excess bone.

★ Allow to dry for 24 hours and place on a flat-frosted cupcake.

CUTE CUPCAKE TOPPERS

Cute! Cute! Cute!
Adorable little additions to a girl's best friend...cupcakes!

TOOLS AND MATERIALS

Knife or blade tool and rolling pin

Pastel yellow, white and black sugarpastes

Pink jellybean

Edible glue and brush

Clingfilm

THE HAMSTER

HOW TO MAKE

STEP 1

★ Roll 3 cm (1¼-inch) and 3 mm (⅛-inch) balls of pastel yellow sugarpaste. Also roll a 7 mm (¼-inch) ball of white sugarpaste and flatten it with your finger to create the face.

★ Mould the hamster's body by placing your finger on the ball and rolling it back and forth.

STEP 2

★ Cut the small ball of yellow sugarpaste in half and roll into two balls. Place each ball under some clingfilm and press one side flat with your finger. Remove the clingfilm and curl the thin side to create an ear; repeat with the other half.

★ Roll two small eyes from black sugarpaste and cut the jellybean in half to create the nose.

STEP 3

★ Glue the face, eyes, nose and ears to the hamster. Indent the body with a blade tool to create fore and hind legs.

★ Allow to dry and place on a frosted cupcake.

TOOLS AND MATERIALS

Knife or blade tool and rolling pin

4.5 cm (1¾-inch) circle cutter

Pastel pink and pastel yellow sugarpastes

Flower shaper tool

Cocktail stick and skewer

Any metal piping tip

Edible glue and brush

THE PONY

HOW TO MAKE

STEP 1

★ Roll out a small amount of white sugarpaste and cut out a 4.5 cm (1¾-inch) diameter circle.

★ Roll out a 2.5 cm (1-inch) ball of pastel yellow sugarpaste and mould into a pony's head shape.

★ Roll out a small amount of pastel yellow sugarpaste and cut out two small triangles for the ears.

STEP 2

★ Mark eyes with a cocktail stick and indent for the mouth with a piping tip. Add two nostrils with a skewer.

★ Using the flower shaper tool, indent the pony's ears and glue to the head.

STEP 3

★ Cut out the pony's mane and face markings, as shown, from the circle. Attach to the pony's head. Using a knife, indent the pony's mane to create the hair effect.

★ Allow to dry and place on a frosted cupcake.

TOOLS AND MATERIALS

Knife or blade tool and a rolling pin

Pale pink sugarpaste

Pale pink buttercream

Wilton no.104 petal tip

Edible glitter

Template for the ballerina's bodice (see page 140)

THE BALLERINA

HOW TO MAKE

STEP 1

★ Use the template (see page 140) to cut out the ballerina's bodice from pale pink sugarpaste.

STEP 2

★ Use a Wilton no.104 petal tip to pipe frills for the ballerina's skirt on the cake. Starting from the centre, work to the edge and back and complete a ring of piped loops.

★ Repeat twice more to create the full skirt.

STEP 3

★ Place the ballerina's bodice into the piped skirt and sprinkle with edible glitter.

These cute little cupcake toppers will soon become any girl's new best friend!

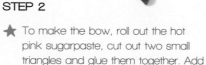

TOOLS AND MATERIALS

A selection of pink, yellow, lilac, hot pink and black sugarpastes

Knife or blade tool and a rolling pin

Paintbrush and edible glue

BLUSH

HOW TO MAKE

STEP 1

★ Roll out a 4 cm (1½-inch) ball of pink sugarpaste and roll into a tear shape.

★ Make a cut in the top to make the heart shape.

★ Use your fingers to smooth out the heart shape and any rough edges.

STEP 2

★ To make the bow, roll out the hot pink sugarpaste, cut out two small triangles and glue them together. Add a small ball to the centre and indent the bow using the blade tool or the back of a knife.

STEP 3

★ Take two small balls of black sugarpaste to create the eyes and roll out slightly with your finger to elongate.

★ Glue the bow and eyes to the heart.

★ Allow to dry for at least 12 hours.

TWINKLE

HOW TO MAKE

STEP 1

★ Roll out a ball of yellow sugarpaste to 1.5 cm (½ inch) thick and mark out and cut out a star shape.

★ Use your fingers to smooth out the star shape and any rough edges.

STEP 2

⭐ To make the bow, roll out the hot pink sugarpaste, cut out two small triangles and glue them together. Add a small ball to the centre and indent for the bow using the blade tool or the back of a knife.

STEP 3

⭐ Take two small balls of black sugar-paste for the eyes and roll out slightly with your finger to elongate.

⭐ Glue the bow and eyes to the star.

⭐ Allow to dry for at least 12 hours.

DEWDROP

HOW TO MAKE

STEP 1

⭐ Roll out a 4 cm (1½-inch) ball of lilac sugarpaste and roll into a teardrop shape.

⭐ Use your fingers to smooth out the shape and any rough edges. Pinch the top of the teardrop shape and bend into place.

STEP 2

⭐ To make the bow, roll out the hot pink sugarpaste, cut out two small triangles and glue them together. Add a small ball to the centre and indent for the bow using the blade tool or the back of a knife.

STEP 3

⭐ Take two small balls of black sugarpaste for the eyes and roll out slightly with your finger to elongate.

⭐ Glue the bow and eyes to the drop.

⭐ Allow to dry for at least 12 hours.

DARCY, DOG IN A HANDBAG

Darcy is a fluffy little friend who you can carry with you anywhere!

TOOLS AND MATERIALS

Knife and rolling pin

Pale pink, hot pink and black sugarpastes

Cocktail sticks

7 mm (¼-inch) circle cutter

2.5 cm (1-inch) circle cutter

Ball tool and flower tool

Small pearl ball sprinkles

Edible glue and brush

NOTES ON THE CAKE

A 15 cm (6-inch) round cake covered in pale pink sugarpaste was used. A black ribbon placed around the base and secured with a pin at the back. Cut out paw prints made from black sugarpaste have been glued to the side of the cake while still pliable.

THE HANDBAG

HOW TO MAKE

STEP 1

★ Mould a handbag shape from pale pink sugarpaste that is 5 cm (2 inches) at the base and tapers to 4 cm (1½-inches) at the top.

★ Roll out some hot pink sugarpaste to 3 mm (⅛ inch) thick and cut out two 2.5 cm (1-inch) diameter circles for the pockets. Also cut out three 5 cm (2-inch) strips for the handles and the vertical detail. You will also need to cut out two 15 cm x 7 mm (6 x ¼-inch) strips for the bag's trim.

STEP 2

★ Glue the trim and handles onto the handbag.

★ Cut across the circles, three-quarters of the way up and indent creases in the larger bottom section using a the knife. Invert the top section and glue to the base to create the lid of the pockets. Glue on a small pearl sprinkle as the button.

★ Cut a 5 cm x 7 mm (2 x ¼-inch) strip of hot pink sugarpaste and glue both ends at the centre to create a bow. Add a small rectangle to the centre of the bow and glue to the front of the bag.

★ Mould a small heart from hot pink sugarpaste and attach to the bag with a thin sausage of hot pink to create a tag.

DARCY

HOW TO MAKE

★ Roll out a 2.5 cm (1-inch) ball of white sugarpaste and then mould it into the shape of the dog's head, including a snout and ears.

★ Using a bone tool, indent for the eyes. Indent for the ears using a flower tool. Using a 7 mm (¼-inch) round cutter, indent the lips twice and use the flower tool to create a mouth. Add two small white sugarpaste eyebrows.

★ Glue two black sugarpaste balls in place as eyes and a black sugarpaste triangular nose, pricked twice with a cocktail stick.

★ Using the tip of the knife, fluff the face to create hair all over the head. Use a small piece of hot pink sugarpaste to create a tongue and indent with a vertical line. Glue the tongue into the mouth. Create a bow from hot pink sugarpaste with two small triangles and a tiny ball for the centre. Glue on top of the dog's head.

★ Insert a cocktail stick into the base of the head and then place into the top of the handbag.

★ Leave to dry for 24 hours and place on top of the cake.

PRINCESS

Play fairy godmother and make your little princess's dreams come true with this enchanting cake topper.

TOOLS AND MATERIALS

Mini doll pick

Knife or blade tool

Rolling pin

Cocktail stick and skewer or modelling tool

Small heart cutter

Muffin-sized cupcake and mini-cupcake

Heart sprinkles

Pearl dragées

NOTES ON THE CAKE

A 15 cm (6-inch) round cake covered in pale pink sugarpaste was used, with a hot pink polka-dot ribbon around the base and secured at the back with a pin. Make sure to remove the pin before serving.

THE PRINCESS

HOW TO MAKE

STEP 1

★ Use a cocktail stick to fix a mini cupcake to an upturned cupcake and insert the doll so that the cupcakes form the base of the skirt.

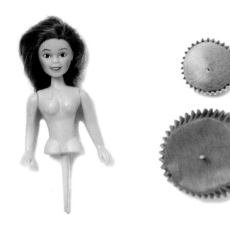

STEP 2

★ Roll out the pink sugarpaste and cut out the bodice shape to fit the doll; glue in place on the doll.

★ Roll out the white sugarpaste and cut out the underskirt and frill strips.

★ Use the technique shown on page 19 to frill the skirt strips.

★ Drape the underskirt over the centre of the doll and glue the frills in place.

STEP 3

★ Roll out the pink sugarpaste, cut out a kidney shape for the skirt and place it around the doll. Glue in place.

★ Use the pearls to decorate the underskirt and neaten the join between the skirt and bodice. Glue heart sprinkles in place.

★ Roll out the pink sugarpaste and cut out a crown shape. This can be done easily by using a small heart cutter.

★ Glue some pearls to the points of the crown and a heart sprinkle to the front and fix the crown in place.

★ Leave to dry for 24 hours.

BOYS' TOYS

These are some rootin' tootin' Wild West cupcakes! And for the table football fan, there's an awesome table football player!

TOOLS AND MATERIALS

Knife or blade tool and rolling pin

Red sugarpaste

White candy stick

Edible glue and brush

THE TABLE FOOTBALL PLAYER

HOW TO MAKE

STEP 1

★ Roll a red sugarpaste sausage that is 2.5 cm (1 inch) x 1.5 cm (½ inch), another sausage that is 2 cm (¾ inch) x 1.5 cm (½ inch) and a 1.5 cm (½-inch) ball for the head.

STEP 2

★ Mould the larger sausage to create the body. Use the blade tool to indent the legs and shorts.

★ Mould the smaller sausage between your fingers to create a base with sharp edges.

STEP 3

★ Gently push the candy stick through the upper body.

★ Glue the base and head onto the body and allow to dry for 24 hours.

★ Place on a frosted cupcake.

TOOLS AND MATERIALS

Knife or blade tool and rolling pin

Brown, black, yellow, blue and red sugarpastes

5.5 cm (2¼-inch) circle cutter

1.5 cm (½-inch) star cutter

A marshmallow cutter

Edible glue and brush

THE FEATHER HEADDRESS

HOW TO MAKE

STEP 1

★ Roll black sugarpaste into three 20 cm (8-inch) long, thin sausages and plait them by folding one over the next. Apply around the edge of a black flat sugarpaste-covered cupcake with glue.

THE COWBOY HAT

STEP 2

★ Roll out the yellow sugarpaste and
  cut out a 6 cm (2¼-inch) diameter
  circle with a cutter; use the same
  cutter to cut out a feather shape.

★ Pinch the end of the feather and
  cut the feather edges with the
  knife. Repeat with red and blue
  sugarpastes to create more feathers.

STEP 3

★ When dry, cut a small hole in
  the back of the cupcake and add
  glue. Carefully insert a feather so
  that it is upright. Repeat with the
  other feathers.

HOW TO MAKE

STEP 1

★ Roll out the brown sugarpaste and
  cut out a 7.5 cm (3-inch) diameter
  circle for the base, lay it flat on some
  Baking parchment and prop up two
  edges with pencils.

★ Roll out brown sugarpaste and cut
  out a 6 cm (2¼ inch) diameter circle
  and place it over a marshmallow
  with a "v" shape cut into it. Mould
  the sugarpaste over the marshmallow
  and trim the edge to create the
  hat top.

STEP 2

★ Roll out a small amount of yellow
  sugarpaste and use a 1.5 cm
  (½-inch) star-shaped cutter to create
  a sheriff's badge. Glue small yellow
  sugarpaste balls to each point of
  the star.

STEP 3

★ Glue the top and bottom of the hat
  together, glue the sheriff's badge to
  front of the hat and place on a
  frosted cupcake.

ARMY

I don't know but I've been told,
for army cupcakes you're never too old!

TOOLS AND MATERIALS

Knife or blade tool and a rolling pin

Green, brown, black, tan and
grey sugarpastes

7 cm (2¾-inch) circle cutter

Edible silver paint

Edible silver lustre spray

White dragées

Mini alphabet craft stamps

Templates for the badge and dog tags
(see page 140)

CAMOUFLAGE

HOW TO MAKE

STEP 1

★ Pinch small amounts of the black,
brown and tan sugarpaste and roll
between your fingers. Then roll flat
with a rolling pin.

STEP 2

★ Roll out green sugarpaste and scatter
the pieces on top. Cover with clingfilm
and roll flat with a rolling pin.

STEP 3

★ Cut out a 7 cm (2¾-inch) circle
from the camouflage sugarpaste
and flat-frost onto a cupcake (see
page 17).

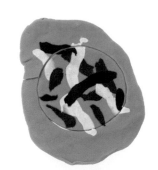

THE DOG TAGS

HOW TO MAKE

STEP 1

★ Using grey sugarpaste, cut out
two dog tag shapes using the
template (see page 140) and create
a thin grey sausage for the chain.

STEP 2

★ Using the alphabet craft stamps,
indent your message or a name
on one of the dog tags.

THE ARMY BADGE

HOW TO MAKE

STEP 1

★ Roll out the green sugarpaste and cut out a badge shape using the template (see page 140).

STEP 2

★ Cut out three grey "V" shapes using a knife and glue to the badge.

STEP 3

★ Glue the badge to a black flat sugarpaste-covered cupcake. When dry, paint the grey stripes with edible silver paint.

STEP 3

★ Assemble the dog tags and chain. Glue the dragées in place to create the chain effect. Apply the edible silver lustre spray and, when dry, place on top of a green flat sugarpaste-covered cupcake.

These freaky little fellas will provide a peculiar twist to any bash!

TOOLS AND MATERIALS

Knife or blade tool and a rolling pin

Red, black, yellow, blue orange, white and purple sugarpaste

Small paintbrush with either a little water or edible glue

Black edible-ink pen

Two small purple sweets

ROYSTON THE MONSTER

HOW TO MAKE

STEP 1

★ Roll out some red sugarpaste to 1.5 cm (½ inch) thick and cut into a rectangular shape to create the body. Use your fingers to smooth out the shape and any rough edges.

★ Use the blade tool to mark the legs.

STEP 2

★ Roll a sausage shape in red sugarpaste to create the arms and cut to the right length.

★ Roll out some yellow sugarpaste and cut a small rectangle for the mouth. Roll out a strip of blue sugarpaste and cut out triangles for the teeth.

STEP 3

★ Assemble all the parts and glue together adding two small black sugarpaste balls for eyes.

★ Allow to dry for at least 12 hours.

SHARK BITE

HOW TO MAKE

STEP 1

★ Mould a fat sausage shape from orange sugarpaste, tapering it at one end. Use your finger to roll the tapered end and create an indent. Give the shark a pointed nose.

STEP 2

★ Mould two fins from black sugar-paste and attach to the shark with edible glue.

★ Using a knife, cut the base to create two feet.

STEP 3

★ To create the mouth, cut a black sugarpaste triangle, a smaller white sugarpaste triangle and black triangle teeth. Affix the layers with edible glue and attach to the shark.

★ Roll a small black sugarpaste ball to create an eye.

★ Allow to dry for at least 12 hours.

LIGHTNING MAN

HOW TO MAKE

STEP 1

★ Mould a head from a 2.5 cm (1-inch) purple sugarpaste ball and mould the body from a 1.5 cm (½-inch) purple sugarpaste ball.

★ Create a white belly by rolling a small white sugarpaste ball and pushing it into a flat, oblong shape. Glue to the body.

STEP 2

★ Roll a small ball of purple sugarpaste into a sausage shape and cut in two to create arms. Glue between the head and body.

★ Glue two purple sweets to the belly, as feet.

STEP 3

★ Roll out a small piece of black sugarpaste and, with a knife, cut out a lightning shape for his antenna and a cross for his eye. Glue in place.

★ Roll out a small and larger ball of white sugarpaste to create the other eye and the nose and attach with glue.

★ Allow to dry for at least 12 hours.

If you want to rock, skate or just hang out with the cool dudes, then these cupcakes are just for you!

TOOLS AND MATERIALS

Knife or craft knife and rolling pin

White and black sugarpastes

Selection of edible-ink pens, including black

Skewer

Edible glue and brush

THE SKATEBOARD

HOW TO MAKE

STEP 1

★ Roll out the white sugarpaste to a 3 mm (⅛-inch) thickness and cut out the skateboard shape using the template (see page 140). Allow to dry for 24 hours.

STEP 2

★ To decorate the base of the skateboard you can use a selection of edible-ink pens. You can choose any design. Here, the child's name is written in a graffiti effect. Remember to leave room for the wheels.

★ To make the skateboard wheels, roll four 3 mm (⅛-inch) black sugar-paste balls and press with a skewer. Cut out two small black strips.

STEP 3

★ Glue the strips and wheels to the skateboard with edible glue.

★ Allow to dry and place on a frosted cupcake.

TOOLS AND MATERIALS

Knife or blade tool and a rolling pin

Blue, purple, black and orange sugarpastes

Edible glue and brush

Black edible-ink

JUSTIN, THE HIPSTER

HOW TO MAKE

STEP 1

★ Roll out a 1.5 cm (½-inch) ball of orange sugarpaste and shape into a teardrop shape.

STEP 2

★ Model a 2 cm (¾-inch) square from purple sugarpaste to create the body. Smooth any edges with your fingers.

★ Model a black sugarpaste square to match the body size. Use the blade tool or the back of a knife to indent for the feet.

★ Roll a blue sugarpaste sausage shape to create the arms and cut to the correct length.

TOOLS AND MATERIALS

Knife or craft knife and rolling pin

White, red and black sugarpastes

Black edible-ink

Small pearl or white ball sprinkles

Edible glue and brush

Red and yellow frosting

STEP 3

★ Roll out the blue sugarpaste and cut out a 2.5 cm (1-inch) diameter circle. Use the knife to cut out the hair pattern. Glue to the head.

★ Assemble the parts and glue together. Once dry you can draw the face on with an edible-ink pen.

THE ROCK GUITAR

HOW TO MAKE

STEP 1

★ Roll out the white sugarpaste to a 3 mm (⅛-inch) thickness and cut out the guitar shape using the template (see page 140).

★ Roll out the red sugarpaste to a 3 mm (⅛-inch) thickness and use the template again to create the red Stratocaster effect. Glue to the white base.

STEP 2

★ Using black sugarpaste, roll sausages as thin as you can to create three strings about 3 cm (1¼-inches) long each. Glue to the guitar body. Using two small white sugarpaste rectangles, secure the ends of the strings.

★ Using a black edible-ink pen, mark the frets on the neck of the guitar.

★ Glue the ball sprinkles to the head of the guitar and add one at the bottom for the volume button. Allow to dry for 12 hours.

STEP 3

★ Place red and yellow frosting in a piping bag to create a two-tone flame effect (see page 15) and place the guitar on top.

We will rock you! This tattoo-inspired cake topper will hit the bass for any hardcore rocker!

TOOLS AND MATERIALS

A selection of red, grey, yellow, blue and black sugarpastes

Knife or blade tool and a rolling pin

Black edible-ink

Edible silver lustre or edible pearl lustre spray

Silver dragées

Clingfilm

Edible glue and brush

Cocktail sticks and skewers

THE WINGED HEART

HOW TO MAKE

STEP 1

★ Roll out a 5 cm (2-inch) ball of red sugarpaste and roll into a teardrop shape. Make a cut in the top to make the heart shape. Use your fingers to smooth out the heart shape and any rough edges. Insert two skewers into the bottom of the heart.

THE GUITAR AND ROSE

STEP 2

★ Roll out the grey sugarpaste to 7mm (¼ inch) thick and use the template on page 141 to cut out the two wing shapes. Use your fingers to smooth out any rough edges on the wings.

★ Use the blade to mark out and indent the wing pattern.

★ Cut away the tip of the wings to produce the feather effect. Allow to dry before spraying/painting silver. When the paint is dry, glue the wings to the heart.

★ Roll out some yellow sugarpaste. Cut a strip for the rock banner and glue in place across the heart. Once dry, write 'ROCK' with black edible ink.

HOW TO MAKE

★ Roll out the black sugarpaste and cut out the guitar handle using the template on page 140. Insert a cocktail stick into the handle, use a knife to indent the lines to represent the strings and glue silver dragées to the end of the handle.

★ Roll nine 8 mm (⅓-inch) blue sugarpaste balls. Place them between layers of clingfilm and press each ball with your finger in an outwards-circling motion to create petals. Remove the clingfilm. Curl one of the petals around itself to create the centre of the bud.

★ Now add three petals around the centre and then another five petals to form a second layer. Curl the edges of the outer petal over with your finger. Trim any excess at the base.

★ Leave to dry for at least 24 hours. When all the parts are dry, assemble together on the cake.

Get the girls together and head straight for these cupcakes!

TOOLS AND MATERIALS

Knife or blade tool and rolling pin

Skewer

Black and pastel pink sugarpastes

Edible glue and brush

THE HAIR STRAIGHTENERS

HOW TO MAKE

STEP 1

★ Roll a 6.5 cm (2½-inch) long sausage out of black sugarpaste. Using a knife, cut the sausage almost in half lengthwise and split to create the hair straightener's shape.

STEP 2

★ Roll out a small piece of pastel pink sugarpaste to 3 mm (⅛ inch) thick and cut out two small rectangles that are 2.5 cm (1 inch) long and glue to the hair straighteners to create the ceramic plates.

★ Indent the end of the hair straighteners with the round end of a skewer to denote the hinge.

STEP 3

★ Allow to dry for 24 hours and place on a frosted cupcake.

★ Roll a thin sausage out of black sugarpaste to create the cord and add to the cupcake whilst still pliable.

TOOLS AND MATERIALS

Knife or blade tool and rolling pin

2.5 cm (1-inch) and 1 cm (½-inch) circle cutters

Skewer

Pastel pink, hot pink and grey sugarpastes

Edible glue and brush

THE MP3 PLAYER

HOW TO MAKE

STEP 1

★ Roll out the pale pink sugarpaste to 7 mm (¼ inch) thick and cut out a 5.5 cm (2¼-inch) by 3 cm (1¼-inch) rectangle. Smooth the corners with your fingers.

STEP 2

★ To make the button, roll out a small piece of hot pink sugarpaste, cut out a 2.5 cm (1-inch) circle and then indent it with the 1.5 cm (½-inch) circle cutter.

★ Roll out a small piece of grey sugarpaste and cut out a 2.5 cm (1-inch) by 2 cm (¾-inch) rectangle for the screen.

★ Roll two small 7 mm (¼-inch) pastel pink sugarpaste balls and pinch the tops to create the earphones. Using a skewer, create a small hole in the tip where the wire will fit.

★ Glue the button and screen to the base and allow to dry for 24 hours.

STEP 3

★ Roll out two thin sausages to create the wires. Place the base and earphones onto a frosted cupcake and, while the sugarpaste is still soft, position the wires from the earphones onto the back of the MP3 player.

HIPPIE CHICK

Spread peace and love with these funky hippie-chick cake and cupcakes.

TOOLS AND MATERIALS

Knife or blade tool and rolling pin

Skewer and cocktail stick or no.3 modelling tool

Brown, hot pink, pale pink and green sugarpastes

Edible glue and brush

Wire

Small flower cutter

Heart cutter or heart template

5 cm (2-inch) circle cutter

3 mm (⅛-inch) circle cutter

THE OWL

HOW TO MAKE

STEP 1

★ Roll a 5 cm (2-inch) ball of brown sugarpaste into a pear shape and pinch two ear shapes.

★ Cut two triangles from hot pink sugarpaste and cut two slightly smaller triangles from pale pink sugarpaste. Glue the smaller triangles to the larger triangles to make the ears.

★ Cut two hot pink sugarpaste circles for the eyes, then cut two slightly smaller pale pink circles and two even smaller brown circles. Cut a small wedge out of the brown circles and assemble the eyes. Roll a small ball of pale pink sugarpaste and add to the eyes.

★ Cut a green sugarpaste triangle for the beak.

STEP 2

★ For the feet, roll a 1.5 cm (½ inch) ball from pale pink sugarpaste and cut in half, roll into a sausage shape and use a knife or blade tool to mark two indents for the claws.

★ Use a 3 mm (⅛ inch) circle cutter to mark the feathers across the owl's breast.

THE OWL CUPCAKE

HOW TO MAKE

★ Cut out a 5 cm (2-inch) circle from the pale pink sugarpaste.

★ Use the template on page 141 to cut out the owl shape from brown sugarpaste. Glue to the pink disk. Cut out a 2 cm (¾-inch) circle in brown sugarpaste and use the cutter again to cut two wing shapes.

★ Cut two green sugarpaste circles for the eyes and glue in place. Roll two small hot pink balls and glue to the eyes.

★ Cut a hot pink sugarpaste triangle for the beak and glue in place.

★ Use the 3 mm (⅛-inch) circle cutter to cut pink or green sugarpaste circles and glue around the owl.

★ Leave to dry for 24 hours.

>

THE HEART CUPCAKE

HOW TO MAKE

★ Cut out a 5 cm (2-inch) diameter circle from the brown sugarpaste.

★ Cut out a heart from green sugarpaste and glue to the circle.

★ Use the 3 mm (⅛-inch) circle cutter to cut hot pink sugarpaste circles and glue around the heart.

THE BUTTERFLY CUPCAKE

HOW TO MAKE

★ Cut a 5 cm (2-inch) diameter circle from the pale pink sugarpaste.

★ Cut out four small hearts from the brown sugarpaste and glue to the pink circle.

★ Cut four smaller green and pink sugarpaste hearts and glue to the brown hearts.

★ Roll a hot pink sausage for the butterfly body and glue in place.

★ Cut three small pink balls graduating in size and stick them to the bottom of the wing. Repeat for the other wing.

THE BIRD CUPCAKE

HOW TO MAKE

★ Cut out a 5 cm (2-inch) diameter circle from the brown sugarpaste.

★ Use the template on page 140 to cut out a bird shape from the pale pink sugarpaste and glue to the brown circle. Use a cocktail stick to mark an eye.

★ Use the 5 cm (2-inch) circle cutter to cut out the wings from brown sugarpaste and glue in place.

★ Cut a triangle for the beak from hot pink sugarpaste and fix in place.

★ Use the 3 mm (⅛-inch) circle cutter to cut green or pink sugarpaste circles and glue around the bird.

THE PEACE SIGN CUPCAKE

HOW TO MAKE

★ Cut out a 5 cm (2-inch) diameter circle from brown sugarpaste.

★ Cut a 4.5 cm (1¾-inch) circle from pink sugarpaste and then cut a smaller 3 cm (1¼-inch) circle to create a ring. Glue the ring to the brown circle.

★ Take the 3 cm (1¼-inch) diameter circle, cut away four wedge sections and place into the ring, leaving you with a peace sign.

Let's all go to the lobby and get ourselves a treat!
It's time for a hot dog, popcorn or a cool, refreshing cola!

TOOLS AND MATERIALS

Small scissors

Red and white cupcake cases

Mini white marshmallows

Shop-bought chocolate fudge frosting

Clear boiled sweets

White sugar sprinkles

Candy stick

Pale brown, brown, yellow and red sugarpastes

THE HOT DOG

HOW TO MAKE

STEP 1

★ Create a 4 cm (1½-inch) pale brown sugarpaste oblong and a 2 cm (¾-inch) brown sugarpaste sausage.

STEP 2

★ Place the ice cubes on top of the frosting and insert a candy stick to represent the drinking straw.

★ Sprinkle with white sugar sprinkles.

STEP 2

★ Cut the pale brown oblong to create the hot dog bun and insert the sausage.

THE COLA

HOW TO MAKE

STEP 1

★ Frost the cupcake with chocolate fudge frosting.

★ Using a knife, tap the boiled sweets to break them and create small squares for ice cubes.

MARSHMALLOW POPCORN

HOW TO MAKE

STEP 1

★ Using scissors, cut slits to form a cross in the mini marshmallows.

STEP 2

★ Place on top of a frosted cupcake to create a bucket of popcorn.

STEP 3

★ Create the mustard by rolling a thin yellow sugarpaste sausage and curling it on top of the hot dog along with small flecks of red sugarpaste to represent the ketchup.

This cupcake creation will be perfect for watching that big game with a bunch of friends.

TOOLS AND MATERIALS

20 cupcakes baked in green cases

35.5 x 25.5 cm (14 x 10-inch)
cake board

Green frosting, piping bag and Wilton
no. 233 tip

White sugarpaste

Knife or blade tool and rolling pin

Shop-bought football cake decorations to
include goals and players

Cocktail sticks and white sticky labels

NOTES ON THE CAKE

This cupcake selection can be made
to cater for as many people as you
like. Twenty cupcakes were used
here and they were placed on a
35.5 x 25.5 cm (14 x 10 inch)
rectangular cake board in four rows of
five. If you need to transport this cake,
it's a good idea to dot a small amount
of frosting on the bottom of each
cupcake case, which will act as glue
and keep the cupcakes in place.

FOOTBALL PITCH

HOW TO MAKE

STEP 1

★ Colour the frosting green and place in a piping bag.
Don't add a piping tip and pipe around the entire
edge of the football pitch. Then pipe over any holes
between the cupcakes.

★ Now add the piping tip and start piping the grass
onto the field. If you find that some cupcakes are
lower than others, just infill with extra frosting and
pipe grass over the top. To ensure an even field,
pipe in rows.

STEP 2

★ Roll out some white sugarpaste and cut out 7 mm
(¼-inch) wide strips for the sidelines. Lay the sidelines
over the grass while it is still wet.

★ Position the goal posts and players. You could
also make corner flags with cocktail sticks and
sticky labels.

SURF'S UP!
RADICAL CAKES

Time to carve some killer waves with these ocean-inspired frosting effects, cracker sand and cool surfboards.

TOOLS AND MATERIALS

A selection of white and coloured sugarpastes

Knife or blade tool and rolling pin

Cocktail stick or skewer

Star sprinkles

7 mm (¼-inch) flower cutter/plunger

Edible glue and a brush

Black edible-ink pen

Piping bag and Wilton no.16 tip (or a small star shape)

Blue- and white-coloured buttercream frostings

Digestive crumbs

NOTES ON THE CAKE

A 20 cm (8-inch) round cake covered in water-effect sugarpaste (see page 17) was used. Cut-out waves, made from blue and white sugarpastes were glued around the base of the cake. Applying edible glue to the top of the cake and liberally sprinkling digestive crumbs on top of the cake created sand. Surfboards and the sign in the sand were inserted on the top of the cake and the flip-flops placed in front.

THE SURFBOARD

HOW TO MAKE

STEP 1

★ Roll out white sugarpaste to 7 mm (¼ inch) thick and cut out a large surfboard shape using the template on page 140.

★ Insert a cocktail stick into the base of the surfboard about halfway up the cocktail stick.

★ Decorate the surfboards with a selection of coloured sugarpastes and sprinkles.

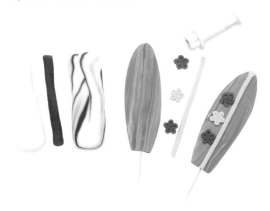

STEP 2

★ Water-effect surfboard cake topper:
   Take a sausage shape of white sugarpaste and add a small sausage of blue sugarpaste. Roll together to create a long sausage and then fold together. Roll again and fold until desired water effect is achieved. Roll out to 7 mm (¼ inch) thick and cut out the large surfboard shape using the template on page 140.

★ Insert a cocktail stick as above and decorate with a pink strip and flowers, using a flower cutter. Secure in place with edible glue.

★ Leave to dry for at least 24 hours.

THE SIGN AND FLIP-FLOP

HOW TO MAKE

★ Create an 'Aloha' sign by rolling out wood-effect sugarpaste (see page 17) to 7 mm (¼ inch) thick and cut out a sign shape using the template on page 140.

★ Make two bases for the sign and insert cocktail sticks through them and up into the main part of the sign.

★ After 24 hours drying, write 'Aloha' in black edible ink.

★ Using a small amount of red sugarpaste, mould two small flip-flop base shapes. Roll out some white sugarpaste as thin as you can and glue to each side and at the centre of the flip-flops.

THE SURFBOARD CUPCAKES

HOW TO MAKE

★ Follow the same instructions as you did to create the cake topper surfboards, but use the smaller surfboard template on page 141 — cocktail sticks are not required.

★ Decorate with a selection of sugarpaste colours and effects.

★ Leave to dry for 24 hours before frosting the cupcakes.

THE CUPCAKES

HOW TO MAKE

★ Frost the cupcake with flat, white buttercream and immediately immerse in digestive crumbs to create the sand effect.

★ Place blue and white buttercream frosting in a piping bag with the no.16 tip. Practice a few strokes to get the correct colour mix and piping effect.

★ Pipe half of the top of the cupcake with waves and then insert the surfboard cupcake topper into the sand.

PIZZA

If you are having a pizza party, why not have pizza for dessert, too?

TOOLS AND MATERIALS

Knife or craft knife and rolling pin

Ball tool and sponge

Beige sugarpaste or marzipan

Pink, brown, green and yellow sugarpastes

2.5 cm (1-inch) circle cutter

Black, red or brown edible-ink pens

Edible brown lustre or paint and brush

Clear alcohol (white rum or vodka)

Yellow frosting

Seedless fruit jam

Black jelly beans

Green sugar sprinkles

Round cake board to fit the number of cupcakes required

THE TOPPINGS

HOW TO MAKE

MUSHROOMS

★ Roll out some beige sugarpaste or marzipan and, using a 2.5 cm (1-inch) circle cutter, cut out a circle. Use the same cutter again to create a crescent shape from the circle. Take a black edible-ink pen and mark the mushroom's gills, using the edge of the tip.

PEPPERONI

★ Roll out a mix of pink and brown sugarpaste to 3 mm (⅛ inch) thick and cut out 2.5 cm (1-inch) diameter circles. Using a ball tool, place the circles on a sponge and indent the pepperoni. Add dots with edible red or brown ink.

HAM

★ Roll out pink sugarpaste to 3 mm (⅛ inch) thick and cut out 2 cm (¾-inch) squares. Place on a sponge and, using a ball tool, roll the ham to create the curled corners.

GREEN PEPPERS

★ Roll out green sugarpaste to 3 mm (⅛ inch) thick and cut out 4 cm (1½-inch) rectangles. Round the edges and bend into a boomerang shape.

PINEAPPLE

★ Roll out yellow sugarpaste to 7 mm (¼ inch) thick and cut a rectangle shape. Using a knife, cut alternating pineapple slices. Indent with the knife.

OLIVES

★ Simply use black jelly beans.

THE PIZZA

HOW TO MAKE

★ Take your required number of cupcakes and place onto a suitably sized round cake board. Arrange them as tightly together as you can.

★ Using a piping bag and any star tip, pipe the yellow-coloured frosting around the edge in a circular motion, working towards the centre, until you fill the pizza. With a spoon, smooth the frosting evenly.

★ Stir the seedless jam in a bowl to make it smoother and place in a piping bag with a star-shaped tip. Pipe the jam around the edge of the crust to create the tomato sauce.

★ Arrange your pizza toppings on the pizza and sprinkle with green sugar to mimic oregano.

★ Take some beige sugarpaste or marzipan and create a sausage that will form the crust. It needs to be long enough to go around the circumference of the pizza. Lay in place.

★ Mix a small amount of brown lustre powder with clear alcohol and paint onto the crust with a brush to create that just-baked effect.

SOUTHERN-FRIED CHICKEN

These delicious chicken drumsticks are presented in a sugarpaste-decorated chicken bucket!

TOOLS AND MATERIALS

Knife or craft knife and rolling pin

White and yellow sugarpastes

15 cm (6-inch) diameter vanilla cake or 12 vanilla cupcakes

500 ml (2 cups) of buttercream frosting

6 digestives

NOTES ON THE CAKE

To create the bucket-shaped cake, the cake was baked in the base of a giant cupcake tin. After a layer of frosting (see page 13), the cake was covered in red sugarpaste and black liquorice sticks were used to trim the top. The sides are decorated with sugarpaste stars and a sugarpaste chicken character. The box for the fries was made with card and a simple box template found online.

THE DRUMSTICKS

HOW TO MAKE

STEP 1

★ Roll out a white sugarpaste sausage that is 6.5 cm (2½ inches) long and, using a knife, split the top and smooth the edges with your fingers to create the chicken bones.

★ To create the fries, roll out yellow sugarpaste to 7 mm (¼ inch) thick and cut long rectangles to mimic fries. Leave to dry for 24 hours.

STEP 2

★ Bake a 15 cm (6-inch) round cake or 12 cupcakes.
When cool, blitz in a food processer until it forms
crumbs. Add the buttercream frosting and blitz again.
The mixture should now be the texture of cookie
dough — dry but able to hold its shape.

★ Mould dough into chicken drumstick shapes about
7.5 cm (3 inches) long. Crush some digestives in a
freezer bag with a rolling pin and place in a bowl.
Roll the chicken drumsticks in the crumbs, insert the
bone into the top and allow to set for three hours.

STEP 3

★ Any leftover dough can be rolled into small balls and
made into popcorn chicken.

★ Assemble the chicken on top of the cake with
the fries.

Before you tee off, you might want to check that nobody's eaten the 18th hole!

TOOLS AND MATERIALS

16 cupcakes baked in green cases

35.5 x 25.5 cm (14 x 10-inch) cake board

Green-coloured frosting, piping bag and Wilton no. 233 tip

Knife or blade tool and rolling pin

Water-effect and marble-effect sugarpaste (see page 17)

Brown, green, yellow and orange sugarpastes

Chocolate cookie finger pretzel stick

5 digestives and Oreo cookies

Shop-bought golfer cake decoration

Edible glue and brush

NOTES ON THE CAKE

This cupcake selection can be made for as many people as you like. Sixteen cupcakes were used here.

THE DECORATIONS

HOW TO MAKE

ROCKS

★ Use the technique on page 17 to create marble-effect sugarpaste and mould it into rocks.

TREES

★ Roll out a 2.5 cm (1-inch) ball of green sugarpaste and mould into a cone. With scissors, snip the cone to create branches, starting at the top and working your way down. You can the insert a chocolate cookie finger or pretzel stick to create the trunk. Repeat to make additional trees and bushes of various sizes. Leave to dry for 24 hours.

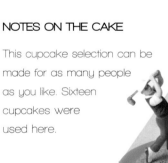

BRIDGE

★ Roll out the brown sugarpaste to 7 mm (¼ inch) thick and cut out two strips that are 7 mm x 8.5 cm (¼ x 3¼ inches). Roll out the brown sugarpaste again to 3 mm (⅛ inch) thick and cut out a 1 x 3-inch (2.5 x 7.5 cm) rectangle.

★ Lay the bridge base over a rolling pin and glue the bridge sides in place. Using a knife, mark the sides to look like bricks. Leave to dry for 24 hours.

DUCK

★ Roll two balls of yellow sugarpaste that are 7 mm (¼-inch) and 1 cm (½-inch). Mould the larger ball as the duck's body along with the tail. Glue the head in place and add eyes with a cocktail stick. Mould a small beak from orange sugarpaste and glue in place.

THE COURSE

HOW TO MAKE

STEP 1

★ Plan where you want to put the green, 18th hole, bunkers, river, dirt and grass.

★ Place five digestives in a plastic freezer bag and crush them with a rolling pin. Frost the cupcakes for the bunkers and dip them into the crumb sand.

STEP 2

★ Roll out the green sugarpaste to 7 mm (¼ inch) thick and cut out the first hole and 18th green. Frost the cupcakes and lay the sugarpaste in place. Create a hole on the 18th green with a cocktail stick.

★ Use the technique on page 17 to create water-effect sugarpaste. Roll to ¼ inch (7 mm) thick and cut out the river. You will need to frost the cupcakes where the river will flow and lay in place.

STEP 3

★ Colour the buttercream frosting green and place in a piping bag with a Wilton no. 233 tip and start piping the grass onto the remainder of the course. If you find that some cupcakes are lower than others, just infill with extra frosting and pipe grass over the top.

★ Finally, add the rocks around the river and put the bridge in place. You can also add the duck, a shop-bought golfer and an 18th hole flag (made from a cocktail stick and white sticky label).

★ Using the same technique as for sand, crush five Oreo cookies (remove the cream first) to create dirt. Frost the desired cupcakes, dunk in 'dirt' and add the trees.

If you know your jack saw from your hacksaw, these DIY-themed cupcakes are the ones for you!

TOOLS AND MATERIALS

Knife or craft knife and rolling pin

Blade tool

Grey, black and yellow sugarpastes

Black edible-ink pen

Cocktail stick

Edible glue and brush

THE HAMMER

HOW TO MAKE

STEP 1

★ Using grey sugarpaste, roll out a 2 cm (¾-inch) long sausage shape for the hammer head.

★ Roll out a thin yellow sugarpaste sausage to create the neck and a black sugarpaste sausage for the handle.

STEP 2

★ Mark the black handle with a cocktail stick to create a dimpled effect.

★ Using a blade tool, indent the head of the hammer and create a split to make the claw of the hammer head.

STEP 3

★ Glue together and allow to dry for 24 hours before placing on top of a frosted cupcake.

THE TAPE MEASURE

HOW TO MAKE

STEP 1

★ Roll out a 1 cm (½-inch) ball of yellow sugarpaste and press with your finger to create a 7 mm (¼-inch) diameter round.

★ Roll out a 7 mm (¼-inch) ball of black sugarpaste and press with your finger to create a circle that will cover the yellow round. Cut a black rectangle that is 7 mm (¼-inch) wide that you can glue three-quarters of the way around the edge of the yellow round.

THE SAW

HOW TO MAKE

STEP 1

★ Roll out the grey sugarpaste to a thickness of 3 mm (⅛ inch) and cut out the saw shape using the template (see page 140). Using the tip of the craft knife, create teeth on the cutting edge of the saw.

STEP 2

★ Cut a rectangle from yellow sugarpaste that is 7 mm (¼ inch) by 2.5 cm (1 inch) to create the tape. Cut out a small grey sugarpaste rectangle to cover the end of the tape measure.

STEP 3

★ Glue the tape measure to the base of the round.

★ Allow to dry for 24 hours before placing on top of a frosted cupcake.

STEP 2

★ Roll out the black sugarpaste to a thickness of 3 mm (⅛ inch) and cut out the saw handle shape using the template (see page 140). Glue the handle to the blade.

STEP 3

★ Allow to dry for 24 hours and place on a frosted cupcake.

Ideal for those loved ones with green thumbs —
this lush green hideaway is a gardener's treat!

TOOLS AND MATERIALS

Knife or blade tool and rolling pin

Cocktail sticks

Grey, green, brown, red, tan, stone and
yellow sugarpastes

Three digestives

Five Oreo cookies

Freezer bag

15 cupcakes baked in brown cases

35.5 x 25.5 cm (14 x 10-inch) cake board

Green-coloured frosting,

Piping bag and Wilton no.233 tip

Plain frosting

7 mm (¼-inch) flower cutter

Edible glue and brush

NOTES ON THE CAKE

This cupcake selection can be made
for as many people as you like. In
this case, 15 cupcakes were used
and placed on a 35.5 x 25.5 cm (14 x
10-inch) rectangular cake board. If you
need to transport this cake, dot a small
amount of frosting to the bottom of
each cupcake to act as glue and keep
them in place.

THE WATERING CAN

HOW TO MAKE

STEP 1

★ Mould the body of the watering can from a 4 cm
(1½-inch) ball of grey sugarpaste, with a taper at the
top. Using a blade tool, mark the two rings around
the bottom and one at the top.

★ With a 7 mm (¼-inch) ball of grey sugarpaste, roll a
sausage shape to create the spout. Ensure that
the base has a diagonal so it will fit the body of
the watering can.

STEP 2

★ Roll out the grey sugarpaste to 3 mm (⅛ inch) thick
and cut a 2.5 cm x 7 mm (1 x ¼-inch) strip for the
side handle. Curl it on its side to make a question-
mark shape. Cut a smaller strip for the top handle.
Again, curl it on its side in a half-moon shape. Leave
to dry for 10 minutes before gluing the parts onto the
body of the watering can.

★ Leave to dry for 24 hours before placing on
the cake.

THE STEPPING STONES

HOW TO MAKE

★ Roll out some stone-effect sugarpaste (see page 17), using tan and white sugarpaste, to 7 mm (¼ inch) thick and cut out seven 2 cm (¾-inch) squares. Leave to dry for 24 hours.

THE HOSEPIPE

HOW TO MAKE

★ Roll out a thin, long sausage of green sugarpaste and curl it around itself to create the hose. Add a grey and yellow sugarpaste nozzle with glue. Leave to dry and then gently place on the cake.

THE RUBBER BOOTS

HOW TO MAKE

★ Roll a 4 cm (1½-inch) ball of green sugarpaste and mould it into one wide rubber boot. Using a blade tool, score down the middle to create two boots (but do not separate them!). Then, using the same tool, create a heel and imprint the tread on the sole. Leave to dry for 24 hours and place on the cake.

THE FLOWERPOTS

HOW TO MAKE

★ Mix some brown and red sugarpastes to create a terracotta colour. Roll it out to 3 mm (⅛ inch) thick and cut out a 2 cm (¾-inch) wide strip. Wrap it around a metal piping tip for the flowerpot shape and trim the edges.

★ Cut out a 1 cm (½-inch) diameter circle and glue to the base. Pierce the bottom with a skewer to create the hole.

★ Cut another strip that is 3 mm (⅛ inch) wide and glue in place to be the rim of the pot.

THE TREES AND BUSHES

HOW TO MAKE

★ Roll out a 2.5 cm (1-inch) ball of green sugarpaste and mould into a cone. With scissors, snip the cone to create branches, starting at the top and working your way down. Insert a cocktail stick into the base so you will be able to place it in the cake. Repeat to make additional trees and bushes of various sizes. Leave to dry for 24 hours.

THE GARDEN TOOLS

HOW TO MAKE

★ Roll out the grey sugarpaste to 3 mm (⅛ inch) thick and cut out a small 'U' shape. Trim the top to create the fork prongs.

★ Roll out a thin sausage of grey sugarpaste and cut the top section in two. Glue the fork into the recess. Add a thin sausage of tan sugarpaste to the base to create a handle.

★ Repeat the process for the trowel, but do not cut prongs into the top.

★ Leave to dry for 24 hours before placing on the cake.

ASSEMBLE THE GARDEN

HOW TO MAKE

PATH

★ Place three digestives in a freezer bag and crush with a rolling pin. The crumbs should resemble sand. Frost the path across the cupcakes and sprinkle the digestives over the frosting. Pat with your finger to secure. Add the stepping stones.

DIRT

★ Use the same technique as for the path, but crush five Oreo cookies (remove the cream first) to create the dirt. Frost the desired cupcakes, dunk them in the 'dirt', and add the trees and flowers.

GRASS

★ Colour the frosting green and place in a piping bag with a Wilton no. 233 grass tip and start piping the grass onto the remainder of the garden. If you find that some cupcakes are lower than others, just infill with extra frosting and pipe grass over the top.

★ Finally, add the watering can, rubber boots, garden tools, flowerpots and hose. Cut out some 7 mm (¼-inch) yellow flowers and arrange them around the garden.

These cake toppers encompass all of a girl's favourite pastimes — shopping, shoes and dresses!

TOOLS AND MATERIALS

Knife or blade tool and rolling pin

Pale pink, hot pink, black and white sugarpastes

5.5 cm (2¼-inch) circle cutter

7 mm (¼-inch) and 8 mm (⅓-inch) circle cutters

3 mm (⅛-inch) flower cutter

Small star cutter

Star sprinkles

Small amount of paper towel

Edible glue and brush

NOTES ON THE CAKE

A 20 cm (8-inch) square cake covered in pale pink sugarpaste was used. A black border and black vertical stripes were added for decoration. The bags and boxes were arranged around the top and the black dress was draped over the edge.

THE SHOPPING BAG

HOW TO MAKE

STEP 1

★ Roll out the pale pink sugarpaste to 3 mm (⅛-inch) thick. Cut out the following shapes:

Two 5 x 4 cm (2 x 1½-inch) rectangles to form the front and back of the bag.

One 2 x 5 cm (¾ x 2-inch) rectangle to form base of the bag.

Two 2 x 4 cm (¾ x 1½-inch) rectangles to form the sides of the bag.

★ Using a knife tool, score the two side panels with a 'Y', as this will allow you to bend the sugarpaste.

★ Leave the parts to dry for 20 minutes. This will allow you to assemble the parts without them flopping around.

STEP 2

★ Once dry, glue all the sides and assemble together. Place a sheet of paper towel in the bag to help it keep its shape.

★ Roll out a small piece of black sugarpaste and cut a thin strip that is 4 cm (1½ inch) long. Whilst wet, shape into a handle and glue on a string of pearl ball sprinkles. Whilst still wet, attach to the front of the bag.

STEP 3

★ Roll out some white sugarpaste as thinly as you can, cut out a rectangle, ruffle it and add to the inside of the bag to create tissue paper.

★ Leave to dry for 24 hours and place on the cake. You can use this technique to make other sized bags and add different decorations, as was done with the blossom bag.

>

THE SHOEBOX

HOW TO MAKE

STEP 1

★ Roll out the hot pink sugarpaste to 3 mm (⅛ inch) thick and cut out the following shapes:

LID

- One 5 x 4 cm (2 x 1½-inch) rectangle for the lid top.
- Two 5 x 4 cm (2 x 1½-inch) rectangles for the long sides.
- Two 4 x 1 cm (1½ x ½-inch) rectangles for the short sides.

BASE

- One 5 x 2.5 cm (2 x 1-inch) rectangle for the base.
- Two 5 x 2 cm (2 x ¾-inch) rectangles for the long sides.
- Two 2.5 x 2 cm (1 x ¾-inch) rectangles for the short sides.

★ Leave the parts to dry for 20 minutes. This will allow you to assemble the parts without them flopping around.

★ Once dry, glue all the sides and assemble.

STEP 2

★ Roll out a small amount of black sugarpaste and cut thin strips to decorate the lid and sides of the box. Glue in place.

★ Cut out small 7 mm (¼-inch) black circles and 8 mm (⅓-inch) pale pink circles and decorate the lid of the box. Add some tissue-paper sugarpaste (made in the same way as for the shopping bag) and glue in place. Leave to dry for 24 hours before placing on the cake.

THE SHOE

HOW TO MAKE

★ Using black sugarpaste, mould a shoe. Use a small ball to form the sole and lay it over a pencil to dry to give the arch effect. After leaving to dry for an hour, form a heel, back and toe strap and glue in place. The shoes are painted with icing sugar glaze to make them shine and give a patent effect. Leave to dry before placing on the cake.

THE HATBOX

HOW TO MAKE

STEP 1

★ Roll out the white sugarpaste to 3 mm (⅛ inch) thick and cut out the following parts:

LID

- One 5.5 cm (2¼-inch) diameter circle.
- One 15 cm x 8 mm (6 x ⅓-inch) rectangular strip for the edge.

BASE

- One 15 x 2.5 cm (1 x 6-inch) rectangle.

STEP 2

★ To form the lid, glue the edge strip to the sides of the circle. Leave to dry.

★ To form the base, curl the rectangle around a 5.5 cm (2¼-inch) circle cutter, leave to dry for 24 hours and then remove the cutter.

STEP 3

★ Roll out the black sugarpaste and cut 3 mm (⅛-inch) strips to decorate the rim of the lid, laying them diagonally across the top and vertically around the base. Glue in place and leave to dry for 24 hours.

★ Add some tissue-paper sugarpaste (as for the shopping bag) and place on the cake.

THE BLACK DRESS

HOW TO MAKE

STEP 1

★ Once all the cake toppers are in place on the cake, roll out the black sugarpaste and, using the large dress template on page 141, cut out the dress shape.

STEP 2

★ Add a belt and corsage, using a 3 mm (⅛ inch) flower cutter and glue onto the dress. While still wet, drape over the hatbox. You may need to add some black sugarpaste to the back to provide support.

THE SHOE CUPCAKE

HOW TO MAKE

★ Roll out the black and hot pink sugarpastes to 3 mm (⅛ inch) thick and cut out a shoe shape using the template on page 141.

★ Cut a small square off each heel, change them over and glue in place.

★ Leave to dry for 24 hours and place on a frosted cupcake.

THE DRESS CUPCAKE

HOW TO MAKE

★ Roll out the black sugarpaste to 3 mm (⅛ inch) thick and cut out a dress shape using the small dress template on page 141.

★ Add a belt and flower corsage, using a 3 mm (⅛ inch) flower cutter and glue onto the dress.

★ Leave to dry for 24 hours and place on a frosted cupcake.

LUAU DANCER

Have your guests hulaing to the buffet table to grab some Polynesian-inspired delights!

TOOLS AND MATERIALS

Mini doll pick

Knife or blade tool and rolling pin

Skewer and cocktail stick

Hot pink, yellow orange, skin-coloured and pale gold sugarpastes

Two marshmallows

3 cm (1¼-inch) circle cutter

6.5 cm (2½-inch) flower cutter

Ball tool

Foam pad and forming cup

Edible-ink pen or paintbrush and food colouring

Edible glue and paintbrush

3 mm (⅛-inch) flower cutter

Shredded wheat

NOTES ON THE CAKE

A 20 cm (8-inch) round cake covered in tan sugarpaste was used. The sides have been decorated with chocolate wafer rolls to give the 'tiki hut' effect. Digestive crumbs were glued to the top and the edges were decorated with small flowers and sugarpaste shells sprayed with gold lustre.

LUAU DANCER

HOW TO MAKE

STEP 1

★ Insert the marshmallows onto a skewer and your doll pick into the top of the marshmallows.

★ Gently break off some of the shredded wheat and glue to the marshmallow skirt.

>

STEP 2

★ Cut out a 3 cm (1¼-inch) hot pink sugarpaste circle, cut a smaller circle from the middle and cut open the back to make the waistband. Glue in place to cover any untidy edges. Cut out a bikini shape and glue to the doll.

STEP 3

★ Use the skin-coloured sugarpaste to mould the legs to suit the size of your doll, gently push the skewer through the legs, then remove and leave the legs to dry for 24 hours.

STEP 4

★ Using the small flower cutter, cut out the flowers in orange, yellow and pink sugarpaste for the lei. Mark the centre of each flower with the edible-ink pen or paint with the food colouring. Glue the flowers in place.

★ Repeat the process with the medium flower cutter for the hair, waist and cake decorations.

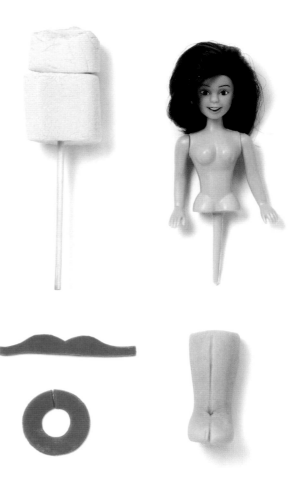

POLYNESIAN FLOWER CUPCAKE

HOW TO MAKE

STEP 1

★ Roll out one of the sugarpaste colours and cut out a flower using the large flower cutter.

★ Place the flower on a foam pad and gently rub the ball tool around the petal edges to thin and curl.

★ Place the flower onto a forming cup.

STEP 2

★ You can paint the centre of the flower with either an edible-ink pen or a little food colouring. If using a colouring paste, try mixing with a little vodka or other clear spirit first.

★ Use a contrasting colour to make the stigma: roll some sugarpaste into a thin sausage, cut it to length and stick in place. Leave to dry for 24 hours.

FRUIT BASKET

If you want to make someone feel better — why not give them a basket of fruit? A sweeter version!

TOOLS AND MATERIALS

Knife or blade tool and rolling pin

Marzipan (or sugarpaste can be substituted)

Green orange, red, yellow and purple food colouring paste

Brown sugarpaste

Serrated cone tool

7.5 cm (3-inch) and 6.5 cm (2½-inch) circle cutters

1 cm (½-inch) star cutter

Cocktail stick

Edible glue and brush

Two cupcakes in each colour baked in green orange, red, yellow and purple cases

Four mini cupcakes

Two plain cupcakes

Black edible-ink pen

NOTES ON THE BASKET

A wicker basket is used to present the marzipan fruit cupcakes. The base of the basket is lined with tissue paper and the cupcakes are placed inside. The grapes and bananas are laid on purple and yellow marzipan, flat-iced cupcakes.

THE APPLE

HOW TO MAKE

★ Mix the marzipan with red colouring paste until you reach the desired colour. Roll it out to 3 mm (⅛ inch) thick and cut out a 7.5 cm (3-inch) circle.

★ Remove a cupcake from its liner, slice it in half through the middle, turn it upside-down and cut four wedges and a hole from the centre. Attach to the top of a cupcake baked in a red cupcake case. Then cover the entire cupcake in frosting.

★ Lay the red sugarpaste circle over the top and gently smooth down to create an apple shape.

★ Using a serrated cone tool or skewer, indent the top to form a small hole. Roll out a small amount of brown sugarpaste, cut out a 1 cm (½-inch) star and place it into the hole.

THE PEAR

HOW TO MAKE

★ Mix the marzipan with green colouring paste until you reach the desired colour. Roll it out to 3 mm (⅛ inch) thick and cut out a 21 cm (½-inch) circle.

★ Place a mini cupcake on top of a cupcake baked in a green case. Cover with frosting and then lay the green marzipan over the top and gently smooth down to create the pear shape. Using a serrated cone tool or skewer, indent the top to form a small hole. Using a knife, indent some small lines coming outwards. Roll out a small amount of brown sugarpaste and cut out a 1 cm (½-inch) star and place into the hole.

★ Take a small piece of brown sugarpaste, mould a stalk and imprint the top with the serrated cone tool or a skewer. Glue into the hole at the top of the pear.

THE ORANGE

HOW TO MAKE

★ Mix the marzipan with a small amount of orange colouring paste until you reach the desired colour. Roll it out to 3 mm (⅛ inch) thick and cut out a 21 cm (½-inch) circle.

★ Place a tablespoon (15 ml) of frosting on top of a cupcake baked in an orange case. Lay the orange sugarpaste circle over the top and gently smooth down to create an orange shape.

★ Using a serrated cone tool or skewer, indent the top to form a small hole. Roll out a small amount of green sugarpaste, cut out a 1 cm (½-inch) star and glue it into the hole.

★ Using a cocktail stick, indent small holes all over the orange to create a peel effect.

THE BANANAS

HOW TO MAKE

★ Mix the marzipan with yellow colouring paste until you reach the desired colour. Roll a sausage about 2 cm (¾ inch) thick and 15 cm (6 inches) long.

★ To form the banana, pinch the top to make the stalk. Use your fingers along the length to mould the ridges of the banana. Using a serrated cone tool or skewer, imprint the top of the stalk. Repeat four times to make a bunch of bananas. Leave to dry for 24 hours.

★ When dry, you can draw the markings on the banana with a black edible-ink pen, along the ridges at the tip and the stalk.

THE GRAPES

HOW TO MAKE

★ Mix the marzipan with purple colouring paste until you reach the desired colour. Roll out a long sausage about 2 cm (¾ inch) thick and cut off 2 cm (¾-inch) pieces. Roll each piece into individual grapes and taper the tops slightly.

★ Arrange the grapes into a bunch pattern and glue into place.

★ Take a small piece of brown sugarpaste, mould a stalk and imprint the top with the serrated cone tool or a skewer. Glue into a gap at the top of the bunch of grapes. You can also paint the finished grapes with icing sugar glaze to make them glossy. Leave to dry for 24 hours.

SUNFLOWER BOUQUET

These sunny flowers will brighten anyone's day and are a perfect way to say thank you!

TOOLS AND MATERIALS

15 cm (6-inch) polystyrene craft ball

15 cm (6-inch) diameter plant pot

16 cupcakes baked in brown cases

Floral tape or a hot glue gun

Colourful tissue paper

Piping bag with white frosting and a Wilton 1M/2110 tip

Piping bag with yellow frosting and a Wilton no. 352 tip

16 3 cm (1¼-inch) round chocolate mints

Cocktail sticks

THE SUNFLOWER BOUQUET

HOW TO MAKE

STEP 1

★ Fix a 15 cm (6-inch) polystyrene craft ball into a suitably sized plant pot, either by taping or using a hot glue gun. (You can cover the craft ball in a colourful tissue paper if required before securing.)

STEP 2

★ Starting at the top and in the centre, insert a cocktail stick to secure the first cupcake. Now work around and insert six more cupcakes and then a final ring around the bottom.

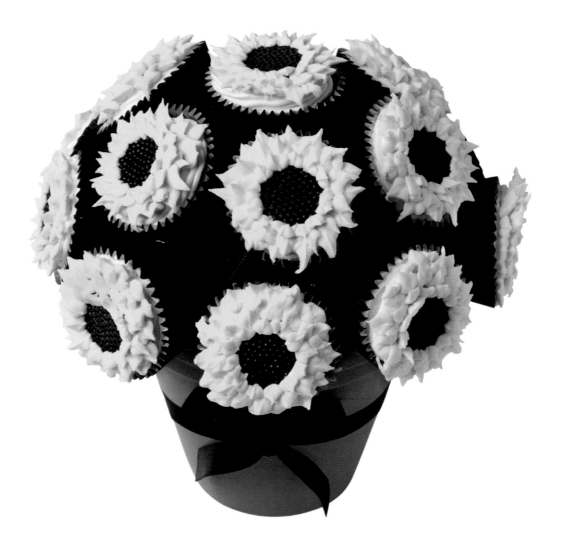

STEP 3

★ Take a cupcake off, pipe a single layer of frosting and insert a round chocolate mint in the centre. Now pipe the yellow petals using the no. 352 piping tip. Pipe a ring of petals around the edge of the chocolate. Then pipe a second ring and a third.

★ Return the cupcake to the bouquet and repeat the process until all the cupcakes are piped. Add more cocktail sticks to secure any loose cupcakes.

A cupcake can be decorated with almost anything; these cakes are ideal for artists, needle-crafters and for special occasions.

TOOLS AND MATERIALS

Knife or craft knife and rolling pin

White, hot pink, pink, tan, yellow and grey sugarpastes

Skewer

Edible glue and brush

THE PALETTE

HOW TO MAKE

STEP 1

★ To create the paintbrush, roll a sausage of hot pink sugarpaste that is 2.5 cm (1 inch) long with a pointed end. To the flat end add a small ball of yellow sugarpaste.

★ To create the bristles, roll a small ball of grey sugarpaste and add an even smaller ball of hot pink. Pinch between your fingers to create a cone shape. Indent with a knife to create a bristle effect. Glue to the top of the paintbrush.

STEP 2

★ Roll out the white sugarpaste to a thickness of 3 mm (⅛ inch) and cut out the artist's palette using the template (see page 140). Using the skewer, create the thumbhole.

STEP 3

★ To make the gradating paint effect, start with a small white ball of sugarpaste and pinch it with your fingers to look like a drip of paint. Then mix the white and hot pink sugarpastes to create different shades and finish with a hot pink drip. Glue to the palette and add the paintbrush.

★ Allow to dry and place on a frosted cupcake.

THE SEWING KIT

HOW TO MAKE

STEP 1

★ To make the spool of thread take a 1 cm (½-inch) ball of tan sugarpaste and mould a cylinder shape that is 1 cm (½ inch) long.

★ Roll two 7 mm (¼-inch) balls of tan sugarpaste and flatten them with your finger to create the ends of the spool. Glue in place.

STEP 2

★ Take a 1 cm (½-inch) ball of pink sugarpaste and roll it into a long sausage, as thin as you can make it. Wrap around the spool to create a thread effect. Leave the end to curl.

STEP 3

★ To make the buttons, roll 8 mm (⅓-inch) balls in hot pink and yellow sugarpastes and flatten with your finger. Use a skewer to indent the buttonholes.

★ To make the needle, roll a 7 mm (¼-inch) ball of grey sugarpaste into a sausage with a point. Curl the other end over and secure with glue to create the eye of the needle.

★ Allow to dry and carefully place on a frosted cupcake.

TOOLS AND MATERIALS

Knife or blade tool and rolling pin

6.5 cm (2½-inch) heart-shaped cutter

Cocktail stick and skewer

Black and pale yellow sugarpaste

Gold edible paint

Gold edible lustre spray

Gold edible glitter

7 mm (¼-inch) flower cutter

Black dragées

Edible glue and brush

THE MASKS

HOW TO MAKE

STEP 1

★ Roll out the black sugarpaste (or gold for the gold mask) to a thickness of 3 mm (⅛ inch) and cut out a large heart shape. Use the cutter again to cut away the top as shown.

★ Using a knife, cut out two eyeholes. Using a skewer, gently press the sugarpaste to create a nose.

★ Gently lay over a rolling pin and allow to dry for 24 hours.

STEP 2

★ **For the black mask:** Using edible gold paint, design a curly decoration on the mask. Sprinkle with gold edible glitter. Allow to dry and place on a frosted cupcake.

★ **For the gold mask:** Using edible gold spray, cover the mask. Allow to dry and, using black food colouring, paint swirls on the mask. Roll out a small piece of black sugarpaste and cut out two flowers. Glue black dragées to the centre of the flowers and glue them to the mask. Sprinkle with gold edible glitter. Allow to dry and place on a frosted cupcake.

CELEBRATIONS AND THANK YOUS

Say thanks, celebrate a new home or show your appreciation for a teacher with these cupcake designs.

TOOLS AND MATERIALS

Knife or blade tool and rolling pin

Black, stone, green and yellow sugarpastes

Marble sugarpaste (mix white and black to create a marbled effect)

Cocktail stick and skewer

Edible glue and brush

THE NEW HOME CUPCAKE

HOW TO MAKE

STEP 1

★ Roll out the black sugarpaste to a thickness of 3 mm (⅛ inch) and cut out a rectangle that is 2 x 4 cm (¾ x 1½ inch).

★ Cut out three marble sugarpaste rectangles to surround the black door. Make the top larger and cut the edges to a point to create the lintel.

STEP 2

★ Using the blade tool, indent the door with two rectangles and two squares. Also mark the lintel with four horizontal lines.

★ Roll out the marble sugarpaste and cut out a rectangle and flowerpots.

★ Roll out a 1 cm (½-inch) ball of green sugarpaste and cut in two. Using the cocktail stick, fluff the green sugarpaste to create bushes.

STEP 3

★ Using a small amount of yellow sugarpaste, cut out a rectangle for the letter box and indent. Roll a small piece of yellow between your fingers and create a door knocker, add a ball of sugarpaste to the join.

★ Glue the components together and allow to dry for 24 hours. Place on a frosted cupcake.

TOOLS AND MATERIALS

Knife or craft knife and rolling pin

Red, green, black, white and yellow sugarpastes

Skewer

Edible glue and brush

THE BLACKBOARD

HOW TO MAKE

STEP 1

★ Roll out black sugarpaste to a thickness of 3 mm (⅛ inch) and cut out a rectangle that is 2.5 x 4 cm (1 x 1½ inches).

★ Roll out white sugarpaste to 3 mm (⅛ inch) thick and cut out a long thin strip that is 3 mm (⅛-inch) wide.

STEP 2

★ Using edible glue, paint the numbers 1, 2 and 3 onto the blackboard and then lay the white sugarpaste strip in place over the numbers, trimming any excess.

STEP 3

★ Roll a sausage of white sugarpaste that is 2 cm (¾-inch) long to create the chalk. Allow to dry and place on a frosted cupcake.

THE APPLES AND CRAYONS

HOW TO MAKE

STEP 1

★ To create the apple, roll a 7 mm (¼-inch) ball of red sugarpaste and add a small ball of green sugarpaste. Roll out another small piece of green sugarpaste and cut out two small leaves.

★ With a small ball of black sugarpaste, create a stalk.

★ Using a skewer, indent the top of the apple. Glue in the leaves first and then the stalk.

STEP 2

★ To create the crayon, take a 7 mm (¼-inch) ball of yellow sugarpaste and roll it into a sausage shape that is 4 cm (1½ inch) long and mould it to a point.

STEP 3

★ Roll out a small amount of black sugarpaste into the thinnest sausage you can. Glue two strips of this around the crayon at both ends.

★ Take another small ball of black sugarpaste and mould an oblong about 2 cm (¾ inch) long to create the crayon's label. Glue in place.

★ Repeat the process to make a green crayon.

★ Allow to dry and place on a frosted cupcake.

CASINO NIGHT

There's no need to bluff with these casino-themed cupcakes. They're the real deal!

TOOLS AND MATERIALS

Plastic cocktail glass

Knife or craft knife and rolling pin

Red, green, white and black fondants

1½-inch (4 cm) circle cutter

¾-inch (2 cm) circle cutter

1-inch (2.5 cm) circle cutter

Black edible-ink pen

Edible glue and brush

Clear hard candies

Candy sticks

Green and white sugar sprinkles

THE DICE

HOW TO MAKE

STEP 1

★ Roll out the white fondant to ¾ inch (2 cm) thick and cut out two ¾-inch (2 cm) cubes.

★ Sharpen the edges by pinching with your fingers.

STEP 2

★ While the fondant is still wet, use the black edible-ink pen to mark the dots on the dice.

STEP 3

★ Allow to dry and place on a frosted cupcake along with green sugar sprinkles.

THE POKER CHIPS

HOW TO MAKE

STEP 1

★ Roll the red fondant out to a thickness of ¼ inch (7 mm) and, using a 1½-inch (4 cm) circle cutter, cut out a circle. Indent the chip with a ¾-inch (2 cm) circle cutter.

STEP 2

★ Roll out the black fondant to a thickness of ⅛ inch (3 mm) and cut out a 1½-inch (4 cm) diameter circle. From the circle's center cut out another ¾-inch (2 cm) circle.

★ Cut this black ring into eight equal segments. Take four of these segments and glue them to the outer ring of the red fondant chip.

★ Repeat the whole process with green fondant to create a green chip.

THE COCKTAIL

HOW TO MAKE

STEP 1

★ To make the lime slice, roll out the green sugarpaste to 3 mm (⅛ inch) thick and, using a 4 cm (1½-inch) circle cutter, cut out a circle. Using the 2.5 cm (1-inch) cutter, indent an inner ring and, using a knife lines for the pulp. Allow to dry for 24 hours.

STEP 2

★ Paint edible glue around the rim of the cupcake case and dunk into a pile of white sugar sprinkles. Frost the cupcake with green frosting.

STEP 3

★ Cut some clear boiled sweets with a knife to create ice. Add to the frosted cupcake along with a candy stick for a straw and the lime slice.

★ Place the cupcake in the plastic cocktail glass to present.

STEP 3

★ Allow to dry and place on a frosted cupcake along with green sugar sprinkles.

RED, WHITE AND BLUE STARS

These vintage-style cupcakes are a superb addition to any festival or celebration.

TOOLS AND MATERIALS

Knife or blade tool and rolling pin

Red, white and blue sugarpastes

6.5 cm (2½-inch), 5 cm (2-inch) and 2.5 cm (1-inch) circle cutters

Cocktail stick or skewer

5.5 cm (2¼-inch), 4 cm (1½-inch), 2 cm (¾-inch) and 1 cm (½-inch) star cutters

Red, white and blue star sprinkles

White dragées

Edible glue and brush

THE ROSETTE

HOW TO MAKE

STEP 1

★ Roll out the red sugarpaste and cut out a 6.5 cm (2½-inch) diameter circle. Use a 1.5 cm (½-inch) star cutter to cut out a star. Also, cut out a 5 x 1.5 cm (2 x ½-inch) rectangle and cut out a triangle from one end.

★ Roll out the blue sugarpaste and cut out a 5 cm (2-inch) diameter circle and a ribbon as above.

★ Roll out the white sugarpaste and cut out a 2.5 cm (1-inch) circle and another ribbon as above.

STEP 2

★ Take a skewer and place it over the edge of the red and blue circles and gently roll up and down, to create the frill detail (see page 19 for technique).

STEP 3

★ Glue the components together and allow to dry for 24 hours. Place on a frosted cupcake.

THE TRIPLE STAR

HOW TO MAKE

STEP 1

★ Roll out the three sugarpaste colours and cut out a 5.5 cm (2¼-inch) star from the red sugarpaste, a 4 cm (1½-inch) star from the white sugarpaste and a 2 cm (¾-inch) star from blue sugarpaste.

STEP 2

★ Glue together and allow to dry for 24 hours. Place on a frosted cupcake.

THE BUNTING

HOW TO MAKE

STEP 1

★ Cut out triangle shapes from blue and white sugarpaste.

STEP 2

★ Glue onto a red flat-iced cupcake.

★ Glue red, white and blue star sprinkles onto the flags.

STEP 3

★ Glue white dragées along the top of the bunting.

You will find yourself hopping crazy for these cute Easter cupcakes!

TOOLS AND MATERIALS

Knife or craft knife and rolling pin

Pastel green, blue, yellow, pink orange and hot pink sugarpastes

7 mm (¼-inch) circle cutter

Black edible-ink pen

Edible glue and brush

Jelly beans

THE EGGS

HOW TO MAKE

STEP 1

★ Roll out the pale green sugarpaste to 3 mm (⅛ inch) thick and cut out an egg shape using the template (see page 140).

★ Using a 7 mm (¼-inch) circle cutter, cut out five circles in a selection of pastel colours.

STEP 2

★ Glue the circles randomly to the egg, ensuring that some cross over the edge, trimming the excess.

★ When dried, place on top of a frosted cupcake.

THE CHICKS

HOW TO MAKE

STEP 1

★ Roll out the pale yellow sugarpaste to a thickness of 3 mm (⅛ inch) and cut out the egg shape using the template (see page 140).

★ Roll a 8 mm (⅓-inch) ball of yellow sugarpaste, flatten with your finger and cut in two to create wings.

STEP 2

★ Glue the wings to the sides of the chick's body.

★ Cut out a small orange triangle to create the beak and glue in place.

STEP 3

★ Mark the chick's eyes with a black edible ink.

★ When dried, place on top of a frosted cupcake.

THE BUNNY

HOW TO MAKE

STEP 1

★ Roll out the pale pink sugarpaste to a thickness of 3 mm (⅛ inch) and cut out two bunny shapes using the template (see page 140).

STEP 2

★ Take one of the bunny cutouts and cut halfway across the head to create the bunny's feet.

★ Roll a small hot pink ball of sugarpaste and glue in place for the bunny's nose. Mark the bunny's eyes with black edible ink.

★ Create a carrot by cutting out a small triangle of orange sugarpaste and adding a green sugarpaste serrated top.

STEP 3

★ When dried, assemble the head and feet on a frosted cupcake along with jelly beans at his belly and the carrot.

It's Hallowe'en! Beware this spooky witch doesn't cast a spell on you! And watch out for the ghost!

TOOLS AND MATERIALS

Knife or blade tool and rolling pin

Black, green, orange, white and purple sugarpastes

Edible glue and brush

THE WITCH'S HAT

HOW TO MAKE

STEP 1

★ Roll a 2.5 cm (1-inch) ball of black sugarpaste and mould the top into the point of the hat.

STEP 2

★ Roll out the black sugarpaste to 3 mm (⅛ inch) thick and cut out a 4 cm (1½-inch) circle.

STEP 3

★ Glue together the circle and hat point and allow to dry for 24 hours. Place on a frosted cupcake.

THE WITCH'S LEGS

HOW TO MAKE

STEP 1

★ Roll out the black sugarpaste and cut out two witch's boots using the template on page 140.

STEP 2

★ Roll the purple and green sugarpaste into 7 mm (¼-inch) wide sausages. Cut the sausages into 7 mm (¼-inch) pieces.

★ Glue the pieces back together in alternating colours to make the witch's legs, which should be about 7.5 cm (3 inches) long.

HOW TO MAKE

STEP 1

★ From a 4 cm (1½-inch) white sugarpaste ball, mould a ghost shape and cut out triangle shapes from its base using a knife.

STEP 3

★ Glue the witch's boots to the legs and allow to dry for 24 hours.

★ Insert into a frosted cupcake.

STEP 3

★ Allow to dry for at least 12 hours and place on a frosted cupcake.

STEP 2

★ Mould two ears from 4 cm (1½-inch) orange sugarpaste balls, one pointing up and the other down and attach to the top of the ghost with edible glue.

★ Roll one small and one larger black sugarpaste ball and attach to the ghost as eyes.

Sleigh bells ring, are you listening?
Revel in these festive treats!

TOOLS AND MATERIALS

5.5 cm (2¼-inch) circle cutter

Black, yellow, red, white and green sugarpastes

Knife or blade tool and rolling pin

Edible glue and brush

SANTA'S BELT

HOW TO MAKE

STEP 1

★ Cover a cupcake with flat, red sugarpaste (see page 17).

★ Cut a 5.5 cm (2¼-inch) circle from rolled black sugarpaste and cut it horizontally into three equal parts. Lay the centre portion over the centre of the cupcake to create Santa's belt.

STEP 2

★ Roll out some yellow sugarpaste to 7 mm (¼ inch) thick and cut out a rectangle that is 4.5 x 4 cm (1¾ x 1½ inches). Using a knife, cut out a smaller rectangle to create the buckle. Apply to the top of the belt.

THE GIFT

HOW TO MAKE

STEP 1

★ Flat-frost a cupcake with white sugarpaste (see page 17).

★ Roll out red sugarpaste to 7 mm (¼ inch) thick and cut out three strips that are 7.5 x 1.5 cm (3 x ½ inches) and one strip that is 2.5 cm x 7 mm (1 x ¼ inch). Apply one of the larger strips to the top of the cupcake as the ribbon.

★ Cut the second large strip in half widthwise and cut inverted triangles from one end of each piece to make two tails for the bow.

STEP 2

★ Fold the ends of the third strip into the centre. Create the centre of the bow by pinching the bow and applying the centre strip, securing at the back with glue. Attach to the top of the ribbon with glue.

★ Assemble the bow and tails on the cupcake and glue into position.

THE SNOWMAN

HOW TO MAKE

STEP 1

★ Flat-frost a cupcake with white sugarpaste (see page 17).

★ Roll out the red sugarpaste to 7 mm (¼ inch) thick and cut out four 2.5 cm x 7 mm (1 x ¼ inch) strips. Repeat with the green sugarpaste. Glue the strips together, alternating red and green.

STEP 2

★ After 30 minutes, when dry, cut out two scarf shapes and apply to the top of the cupcake with glue.

★ Roll three 7 mm (¼-inch) balls of black sugarpaste to create the buttons. Apply to the cupcake with glue.

CHRISTMAS WREATH

This festive cupcake wreath makes the perfect centrepiece to any holiday celebration!

TOOLS AND MATERIALS

Knife or blade tool and rolling pin

Red, green and brown sugarpastes

Scissors

Holly leaf cutter

Flower forming cups

Disposable piping bag (end cut with an inverted 'V')

Green frosting

Edible glue and brush

Red berry sweets

Non-edible gold bells

Cake board

THE WREATH

HOW TO MAKE

STEP 1

★ Roll six 1.5 cm (½-inch) brown sugarpaste balls and mould each one into a pinecone. Use scissors to cut the scales on each one. Leave to dry for 24 hours.

STEP 2

⭐ Roll out and cut out 12 holly leaves. Use a blade tool to mark the leaves and arrange on a forming cup. Glue the berry sweets in place and leave to dry for 24 hours.

STEP 3

⭐ To make the bow, cut out two 4 x 12.5 cm (1½ x 5-inch) rectangles from red sugarpaste, fold them over and support them using some paper towel. Pinch the ends together. Cut a 5 x 1 cm (2 x ½-inch) strip of red sugarpaste and wrap it around the bow loop ends. Cut two 6.5 x 4 cm (2½ x 1½-inch) rectangles, cut away an inverted triangle from one end of each and pinch the other end together. Assemble the bow and leave to dry for 24 hours.

⭐ Assemble the cupcakes together in a ring on a cake board. You can use a little frosting on the bottom of each cupcake to fix them in place. Begin frosting with a random leaf pattern. When all the cupcakes are covered, place your dried bow, holly, pine cones and the bells on top of the cupcakes. Always make guests aware of non-edible items.

Get ready for the holidays with Santa's little helpers and these adorable personalised Christmas stockings!

TOOLS AND MATERIALS

Knife or blade tool and rolling pin

4 cm (1½-inch) star cutter

Skin-coloured sugarpaste or marzipan

Green sugarpaste

Hershey's Kisses or similar

Edible glue and brush

Clingfilm

THE ELVES

HOW TO MAKE

STEP 1

★ Roll out the green sugarpaste to 3 mm (⅛ inch) thick and cut out the star shape.

★ Roll out 1.5 cm (½-inch) and 7 mm (¼-inch) balls of skin-coloured sugarpaste or marzipan.

STEP 2

★ Mark eyes and a mouth with the cocktail stick or indent the mouth with a piping tip. Add a small ball of sugarpaste for the nose.

★ To make the ears, cut the smaller ball of sugarpaste in two, re-roll into balls and place under clingfilm. Flatten down to one side, remove the clingfilm and pinch the flattened side to a point. Glue the ears to the head.

STEP 3

★ Glue the head to the star collar and glue a Hershey's Kiss to the top of the head. Glue to the top of a flat-iced mini cupcake.

TOOLS AND MATERIALS

Knife or blade tool and rolling pin

Red and white fondants

Toothpick and skewer

Black edible-ink pen

White edible glitter

Edible glue and brush

PERSONALIZED STOCKINGS

HOW TO MAKE

STEP 1

★ Roll out the red fondant to ⅛ inch (3 mm) thick and cut out the boot shape using the template on page 140. Also cut out a 3-inch (7.5 cm) long strip of red fondant for the ribbon.

★ Roll out the white fondant and cut out a rectangle that is 1 x ¾ inches (2.5 x 2cm) wide and cut the ends inward.

STEP 2

★ Glue the stocking and ribbon onto a green, flat fondant-covered cupcake and allow to dry for 12 hours.

STEP 3

★ Using a black edible-ink pen, write your required names on the stocking.

★ Sprinkle with white edible glitter.

CHRISTMAS TREE

Time for family and friends to gather around the tree! A fantastic cupcake display – perfect for a large holiday gathering!

TOOLS AND MATERIALS

50 regular sized cupcakes

12 mini-cupcakes

17.5 cm (7-inch) diameter x 38 cm (15-inches) high polystyrene craft cone

Cocktail sticks

225 g (8 oz) red sugarpaste

225 g (8 oz) green sugarpaste

5 cm (2½-inch) circle cutter

Edible glitter

Red or green tissue paper (optional)

Edible glue and brush

THE BAUBLE TREE

HOW TO MAKE

STEP 1

★ Cover your cupcakes with the green and red sugarpaste, so they are flat (as shown on page 17).

STEP 2

★ If you don't want to see any white polystyrene on your finished tower, you can cover it in red or green tissue paper.

★ Start at the bottom of your cone and, using cocktail sticks half inserted into the polystyrene, position your cupcakes around the base of the cone, alternating between the green and red cupcakes.

★ When you have completed the first row, decide on what is the front and position the cupcakes on the second row so that they rest between the two cupcakes below. Go half-way around this time and continue up so that the front looks uniform.

★ Continue the pattern around the back of the cone. As you work your way around, you will find it harder to fit in the larger cupcakes so you can insert the mini-cupcakes into any gaps.

★ When you have finished fixing the cupcakes in place, make sure they are secure. You may need to use extra cocktail sticks on some cakes; these can be pushed through the side of the case and into the cone.

★ To finish, sprinkle some edible glitter over the cupcakes and fix a star decoration to the top of your cone.

HYDRANGEA CENTREPIECE

This fabulous floral table centrepiece is sure to impress your guests! Perfect for a wedding table, where the flowers double as favours!

TOOLS AND MATERIALS

Rolling pin

White sugarpaste

Hydrangea cutter and mould

Edible pearl lustre spray

15 cm (6-inch) polystyrene craft ball

15 cm (6-inch) diameter vase

16 cupcakes baked in white cases

Floral tape or a hot glue gun

Piping bag with white frosting

Wilton 1M/2110 tip

Cocktail sticks

THE BLOSSOMS

HOW TO MAKE

STEP 1

★ Roll out the white sugarpaste to 2 mm ($^1/_{16}$ inch) thick and, using the hydrangea cutter, cut out a single flower.

★ Now press it into the hydrangea mould to create the individual blossom. Repeat twice more and stand the blossoms against each other so that they dry in a three-dimensional shape.

★ You will need 10 blossoms per cupcake. Allow them to dry for 24 hours and spray with pearl lustre spray for a subtle shimmer finish.

STEP 2

★ Fix a 15 cm (6-inch) polystyrene craft ball into a suitably sized vase, either by taping or using a hot-glue gun.

★ Starting at the top and in the centre, insert a cocktail stick to secure the first cupcake. Then work around and insert six more cupcakes and then a final ring around the bottom. You may need to apply additional cocktail sticks to secure any loose cupcakes.

STEP 3

★ Using a Wilton 1M/2110 tip, apply a swirl of white frosting to a cupcake while it is still attached. Immediately apply the 10 hydrangea blossoms, so they are glued to the cupcakes with the frosting.

★ Repeat so that the blossoms cover all the cupcakes. You can also add some extra blossoms to any obvious gaps between the cupcakes.

★ Make sure your guests remove the cocktail sticks before eating.

MINI ROSE BOUQUET

This beautiful bouquet of mini-cupcakes decorated with hand-piped roses is an elegant addition to the top of a wedding cake.

TOOLS AND MATERIALS

10 cm (4-inch) polystyrene craft ball

18 mini-cupcakes baked in silver cases

Cocktail sticks

Skewer

Pink frosting in a piping bag

Wilton no.104 rose tip

NOTES ON THE CAKE

An 18 cm (7-inch) round cake covered in white sugarpaste was used, a pink satin ribbon wrapped around middle and secured at the back with a pin. A pink satin ribbon bow at the front is secured with a diamanté brooch. Remember to remove any non-edible items before serving.

THE ROSES

HOW TO MAKE

STEP 1

★ Slice off the bottom from a 10-cm (4-inch) polystyrene craft ball two-thirds of the way down (a serrated bread knife is ideal for this job). Make a hole in the bottom at the centre with a skewer – this will help to secure it to the cake at a later stage.

★ Starting at the top and in the centre, insert a cocktail stick to secure the first cupcake. You may need to trim the cocktail sticks if they are too long. Now work your way around and insert six more cupcakes and then a final ring around the bottom (as shown).

STEP 2

★ Remove a cupcake and pipe a rose using pink frosting and a Wilton no.104 rose tip (see page 15). Replace on the bouquet, take the next cupcake and repeat the process.

★ You may need to secure any loose cupcakes with additional cocktail sticks.

STEP 3

★ Place the completed bouquet on top of a cake. It can be secured with either a blob of frosting or by placing a skewer in the cake and allowing the sharp end to protrude 5 cm (2 inches) out of the cake. Gently lower the bouquet onto the skewer, making sure it's centred.

★ Ensure that your guests remove the cocktail sticks before eating.

DAISY CUPCAKE TOWER

This cupcake tower is ideal for a wedding or large celebration. The daisies can be made in any colour to match the theme.

TOOLS AND MATERIALS

4 cm (1½-inch) daisy flower cutter

15 cm (6-inch) round sponge cake covered in white sugarpaste on a cake drum

10 cm (4-inch) round polystyrene dummy cake

White and yellow sugarpastes

Cocktail sticks

1 m (3-feet) of 2.5 cm (1-inch) yellow satin ribbon

7 mm (¼-inch) circle cutter

Baking parchment

Edible glue and brush

THE DAISY CAKE

HOW TO MAKE

★ Cover a 15 cm (6-inch) round cake with white sugarpaste (see page 16). Now cover the 10 cm (4-inch) polystyrene dummy cake with white sugarpaste using the same technique. Allow the sugarpaste to dry for 24 hours.

★ When the sugarpaste is dry, insert four cocktail sticks halfway into the base of the polystyrene dummy cake; this will be the top tier. Position it centrally on top of the real cake and insert the cocktail sticks into the cake. Trim the base of each layer with a coordinating yellow satin ribbon and secure at the back with a pin. Remember to remove any pins before serving.

★ Roll out the yellow sugarpaste and cut out lots of 7 mm (¼-inch) circles. Glue them to the top tier of the cake in a polka-dot pattern. If you are not confident doing this freehand, print a polka-dot pattern from the Internet and lay it on the cake. Make a pin prick for each dot to guide you and glue the yellow sugarpaste dots in place.

★ For the base tier, make nine sugarpaste daisies in the same way as you did for the daisy cupcake toppers. Leave to dry for just five minutes and then, while they are still pliable, glue onto the side of the base layer.

★ An acrylic cupcake stand can be used to display the cake; this can be adjusted to fit the number of cupcakes required.

THE DAISY CUPCAKES

HOW TO MAKE

★ Roll out the white sugarpaste to 3 mm (⅛ inch) thick and use a 4 cm (1½-inch) daisy cutter to cut out the petals. Take some yellow sugarpaste, cut out a 7 mm (¼-inch) ball and glue it to the centre of the daisy, pressing flat.

★ Using a palette knife, move the completed daisy to a flat surface covered in Baking parchment. Allow to dry for 24 hours.

★ Once dry, place upright on a frosted cupcake baked in a coordinating yellow case.

WEDDING CUPCAKES

These cupcake designs would complement any wedding with their classic colours and themes.

TOOLS AND MATERIALS

Knife or craft knife and rolling pin

White and black sugarpastes

7 mm (¼-inch) flower cutter

Pearl dragées

Edible glue and brush

THE WEDDING CAKE

HOW TO MAKE

STEP 1

★ Roll out the white sugarpaste to a thickness of 7 mm (¼ inch) and cut out a rectangle that is 5 x 4 cm (2 x 1½ inches).

★ Create a three-tier cake shape by cutting out smaller rectangles for each layer.

STEP 2

★ Roll out a small amount of black sugarpaste to 3 mm (⅛ inch) thick and cut out 3 mm (⅛-inch) wide black strips to create the black ribbon around each layer of the cake.

★ Glue in place with edible glue.

STEP 3

★ Using a 7 mm (¼-inch) flower cutter, cut out two small flowers from the black sugarpaste. In the centre of each flower, glue a small pearl ball sprinkle or a small ball of white sugarpaste.

★ Allow to dry for at least 24 hours and place on a frosted cupcake.

TOOLS AND MATERIALS

White, yellow and green sugarpastes

5 cm (2-inch) heart cutter

1 cm (½-inch) heart cutter

Cake decorating sponge

Paper towel

Edible glue and paintbrush

THE CALLA LILY

HOW TO MAKE

STEP 1

★ Roll out the white sugarpaste to a thickness of 3 mm (⅛ inch) and cut out a 5 cm (2-inch) heart shape. Curl the top curves of the heart over each other and secure them with glue. Add a small roll of paper towel into the resulting funnel so that the flower can dry holding its shape. Leave to dry for 24 hours and then remove the paper towel.

STEP 2

★ Roll out a small amount of green sugarpaste and cut out a 1 cm (½-inch) heart. Curl the green heart around the base of the flower to represent the leaf and glue in place.

★ Roll out a thin sausage of yellow sugarpaste to form the spadix and glue to the centre of the flower. Place a small piece of paper towel underneath to provide support while the spadix is gluing. This can be removed after 24 hours.

STEP 3

★ Once dry, place on top of a frosted cupcake.

TOOLS AND MATERIALS

Knife or craft knife and rolling pin

White and yellow sugarpastes

6.5 cm (2½-inch) daisy or gerbera flower cutter

6.5 cm (2½-inch) diameter terracotta flowerpot (available at garden centres)

Edible glue and brush

THE DAISY FLOWERPOTS

HOW TO MAKE

STEP 1

★ Roll out the white sugarpaste to a thickness of 7 mm (¼ inch) and leave for a few minutes to create a crust. This will help the sugarpaste release from the flower cutter.

★ Using a 6.5 cm (2½-inch) daisy or gerbera flower cutter, cut out the flower shape and place on baking parchment.

STEP 2

★ Take a 7 mm (¼-inch) ball of yellow sugarpaste and flatten it with your finger to create the centre of the flower.

★ Using a ball tool, indent the centre of the flower and then, using a knife or blade tool, indent the outer ring of the flower's petals. Glue to the centre of the flower.

STEP 3

★ Allow to dry. Insert the unfrosted cupcake into a 6.5 cm (2½-inch) diameter terracotta flowerpot (don't force it, you still need to get it out to eat!).

★ Frost the cupcake and, using a spatula, carefully pick up the daisy and place it onto the cupcake, facing forwards.

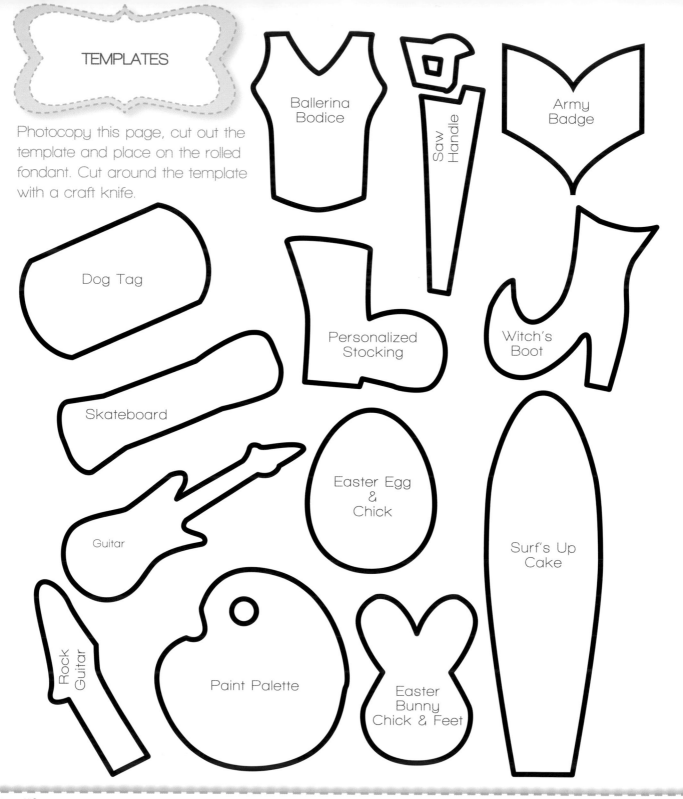

TEMPLATES

Photocopy this page, cut out the template and place on the rolled fondant. Cut around the template with a craft knife.

Ballerina Bodice

Saw Handle

Army Badge

Dog Tag

Personalized Stocking

Witch's Boot

Skateboard

Easter Egg & Chick

Surf's Up Cake

Guitar

Rock Guitar

Paint Palette

Easter Bunny Chick & Feet

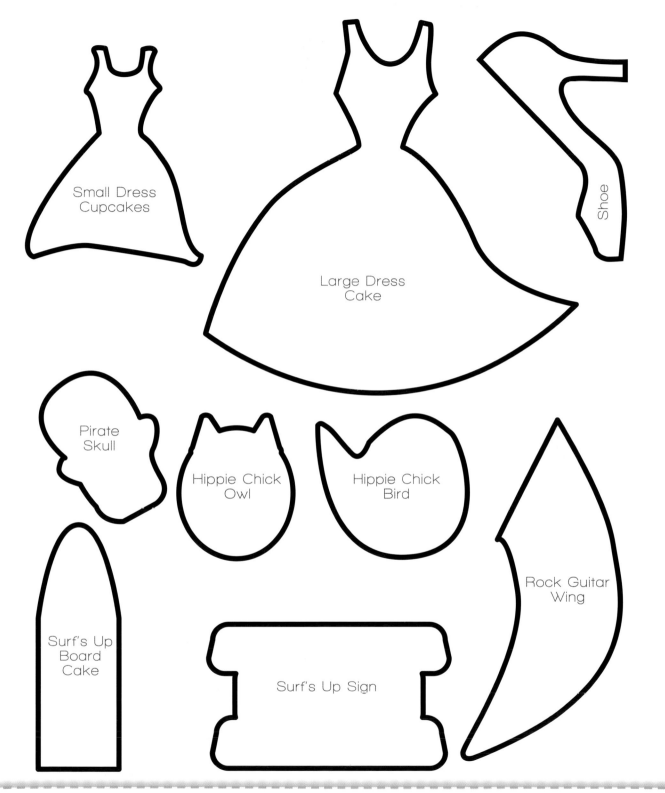

Small Dress
Cupcakes

Large Dress
Cake

Shoe

Pirate
Skull

Hippie Chick
Owl

Hippie Chick
Bird

Rock Guitar
Wing

Surf's Up
Board
Cake

Surf's Up Sign

Index

Suppliers

You can purchase a whole range of equipment and materials, including sugarpaste and cutters, from the following online suppliers.

UNITED KINGDOM

Lakeland.co.uk
Shop online or in their 57 outlets throughout the UK

Hobbycraft.co.uk
Shop online or in outlets all over the UK

Blueribbons.co.uk
Shop online or at their outlet in East Molesey, Surrey

Cakescookiesandcraftshop.co.uk
Shop online

AUSTRALIA AND NEW ZEALAND

Cakedeco.com.au
Shop online

Cakesaroundtown.com.au
Shop online

Thecakeshop.co.nz
Shop online

UNITED STATES AND CANADA

Michaels.com
Shop online or at outlets throughout United States and Canada

Globalsugarart.com
Shop online

Wilton.com
Shop online

Credits

All photographs and illustrations are the copyright of Quarto Publishing plc. While every effort has been made to credit contributors, Quarto would like to apologise should there have been an omissions or errors — and would be pleased to make the appropriate correction for future editions.